EDITIONS

ARMENIAN
BULGARIAN
BURMESE (Myanmar)
CHINESE
DUTCH
ENGLISH
  Africa
  Australia
  Chinese/English
  India
  Indonesia
  Indonesian/English
  Japan
  Korean/English
  Korean/English/
    Japanese
  Myanmar
  Philippines
  Singapore
  Sri Lanka
  United Kingdom
  United States
ESTONIAN
FRENCH
GREEK
GUJARATI
HINDI
HUNGARIAN
IBAN/ENGLISH
ILOKANO
INDONESIAN
ITALIAN
JAPANESE
KANNADA
KOREAN
MALAYALAM
NEPALI
NORWEGIAN
ODIA
POLISH
PORTUGUESE
  Africa
  Brazil
  Portugal
RUSSIAN
SINHALA
SPANISH
  Caribbean
  Mexico
  South America
  United States
SWEDISH
TAMIL
TELUGU
THAI
URDU

THE UPPER ROOM

WHERE THE WORLD MEETS TO PRAY

Sarah Wilke
Publisher

Susan Hibbins
UK editor

INTERDENOMINATIONAL

INTERNATIONAL

INTERRACIAL

33 LANGUAGES

Multiple formats are available in some languages

The Bible Reading Fellowship
15 The Chambers, Vineyard
Abingdon OX14 3FE
brf.org.uk
biblereadingnotes.org.uk

The Bible Reading Fellowship (BRF) is a Registered Charity (233280)

ISBN 978 0 85746 442 2

The Upper Room © BRF 2017

Acknowledgments

The New Revised Standard Version of the Bible, Anglicised Edition, copyright © 1989, 1995 by the Division of Christian Education of the National Council of the Churches of Christ in the USA. Used by permission. All rights reserved.

Scripture quotations taken from The Holy Bible, New International Version (Anglicised edition) copyright © 1979, 1984, 2011 by Biblica. Used by permission of Hodder & Stoughton Publishers, an Hachette UK company. All rights reserved. 'NIV' is a registered trademark of Biblica. UK trademark number 1448790.

Extracts from the Authorised Version of the Bible (The King James Bible), the rights in which are vested in the Crown, are reproduced by permission of the Crown's Patentee, Cambridge University Press.

Extracts from CEB copyright © 2011 by Common English Bible.

Printed by Gutenberg Press, Tarxien, Malta

The Upper Room: how to use this book

The Upper Room is ideal in helping us spend a quiet time with God each day. Each daily entry is based on a passage of scripture, and is followed by a meditation and prayer. Each person who contributes a meditation to the magazine seeks to relate their experience of God in a way that will help those who use *The Upper Room* every day.

Here are some guidelines to help you make best use of *The Upper Room*:

1. Read the passage of Scripture. It is a good idea to read it more than once, in order to have a fuller understanding of what it is about and what you can learn from it.
2. Read the meditation. How does it relate to your own experience? Can you identify with what the writer has outlined from their own experience or understanding?
3. Pray the written prayer. Think about how you can use it to relate to people you know, or situations that need your prayers today.
4. Think about the contributor who has written the meditation. Some *Upper Room* users include this person in their prayers for the day.
5. Meditate on the 'Thought for the day', the 'Link2Life' and the 'Prayer Focus', perhaps using them again as the focus for prayer or direction for action.

Why is it important to have a daily quiet time? Many people will agree that it is the best way of keeping in touch every day with the God who sustains us, and who sends us out to do his will and show his love to the people we encounter each day. Meeting with God in this way reassures us of his presence with us, helps us to discern his will for us and makes us part of his worldwide family of Christian people through our prayers.

I hope that you will be encouraged as you use the magazine regularly as part of your daily devotions, and that God will richly bless you as you read his word and seek to learn more about him.

Susan Hibbins
UK Editor

In Times of/For Help with . . .

Below is a list of entries in this copy of *The Upper Room* relating to situations or emotions with which we may need help:

Anxiety: Mar 2, 5, 27; Apr 11
Assurance: Mar 3; Apr 13
Bible reading/study: Jan 3; Feb 10, 15
Celebration: Mar 29; Apr 30
Change: Jan 23, Feb 10
Church/Christian community: Jan 10, 24; Feb 13, 28; Mar 10, 13; Apr 4, 24
Compassion: Feb 1; Apr 12, 21
Creation: Jan 13, 27; Mar 23, 28
Death/grief: Mar 3, 14; Apr 7
Discouragement: Mar 16; Apr 27
Encouragement: Jan 8, 23, 31; Feb 18, 28; Mar 6; Apr 17, 29
Evangelism: Jan 4; Feb 28
Faith: Jan 2, 18, 31; Feb 18, 24
Family: Mar 7; Apr 17, 30
Financial concerns: Mar 22
Forgiveness: Feb 12; Mar 3
Freedom: Feb 7
Friendship: Mar 15, 16
Generosity/giving: Mar 29
God's goodness/love/grace: Jan 26, 31; Feb 16, 20; Mar 7, 28; Apr 1, Apr 9, 30
God's guidance: Jan 14; Feb 6, 15, 21
God's presence: Jan 20, 23; Feb 2, 5, 13; Mar 17, 22, 31; Apr 8
God's promises: Jan 20; Feb 5, 7
God's provision: Feb 2; Apr 26
Gratitude: Mar 25; Apr 7
Grief: Jan 25, Feb 9, 14
Guidance: Mar 12, 27, 31
Healing/illness: Jan 17, 25; Feb 2, 26; Mar 11, 17; Apr 15, 28
Hope: Mar 6; Apr 16
Hospitality: Mar 15, 24; Apr 21
Joy: Jan 5; Apr 20
Judging: Jan 22, 24, 27

Lent/Easter: Mar 2, 8, 21; Apr 16
Listening/waiting for God: Jan 12, 13, 28; Feb 11, 20
Living our faith: Mar 1, 4, 13, 24; Apr 12, 14, 16
Loss: Apr 14, 25
Making choices: Feb 5
Mission/outreach: Apr 6, 10, 15, 21
New beginnings: Mar 18, 21; Apr 2, 16, 22, 23
Obedience: Jan 2, 6
Praise: Jan 16
Peace: Feb 22
Prayer: Jan 11, 14, 18; Feb 2, 10, 21, 27; Mar 11, 17, 26; Apr 7, 15, 29
Relationships: Jan 19;
Repentance: Jan 19; Feb 12; Apr 2
Salvation: Mar 14; Apr 22
Security: Apr 13
Serving others: Jan 1, 8, 24; Feb 3, 21, 25; Mar 9, 18; Apr 18, 26
Social issues: Mar 22; Apr 24
Spiritual practices: Jan 6, 25, 30; Feb 4; Mar 1, 2; Apr 5, 26, 27
Stewardship: Apr 5
Strength: Jan 1, 26; Feb 20, 26; Apr 9
Struggles: Jan 18, 20, 21, 25; Feb 1, 2, 6, 7, 11, 27
Thankfulness: Jan 2, 8, 16, 21
Transformation: Jan 6, 9; Feb 4, 12
Transitions: Mar 8, 9, 30; Apr 4
Trust: Jan 2, 7, 20; Feb 1, 2, 18; Mar 12, 26, 30; Apr 8, 11, 25
Worldly distractions: Jan 12
Worry: Apr 20

A New Response to Christ's Command

[Jesus] said to them, 'Go into all the world and preach the gospel to all creation' (Mark 16:15).

This instruction was among the final words that the risen Christ offered to his disciples. 'All the world'? Surely, it must have seemed an overwhelming command at the time. But Christ understood the power of the gospel, and his words turned into seeds that continue to be planted around the world today. They certainly are the words that have guided The Upper Room's international ministry, which began soon after its founding in 1935.

In The Upper Room's early years, international missionaries carried copies of the daily devotional to share in their far-flung ministries. Over the decades, we have established editions in 35 languages that are now distributed in 100 countries—and we continue to work to widen and deepen our reach.

In just the past year, we have opened regional headquarters in Buenos Aires, Argentina and Seoul, South Korea. Though we have long had a presence in Latin America and Asia, these offices now permit The Upper Room to be even more responsive to the needs and demands of these global regions. The two hubs join the Upper Room office in South Africa, which opened in 2002 in Johannesburg, South Africa, to serve that continent.

Already, the staffs in our two new offices are beginning to identify new opportunities in ministry so that they can respond with initiatives that are better tailored to these regions' diverse cultures. We're also looking to these outposts for new ideas that will enhance all of our ministries worldwide.

Combined with our ever-expanding array of digital resources, we at The Upper Room are moving that much closer to going into 'all the world'. I invite you to join our prayers that we live fully into Christ's resounding words.

Sarah Wilke, Publisher

Where the World Meets to Pray

Côte d'Ivoire: Every day, *The Upper Room* meditation is read in French on UMC Radio La Voix de l'Espérance (The Voice of Hope). The radio station boasts a listening audience of five million people!

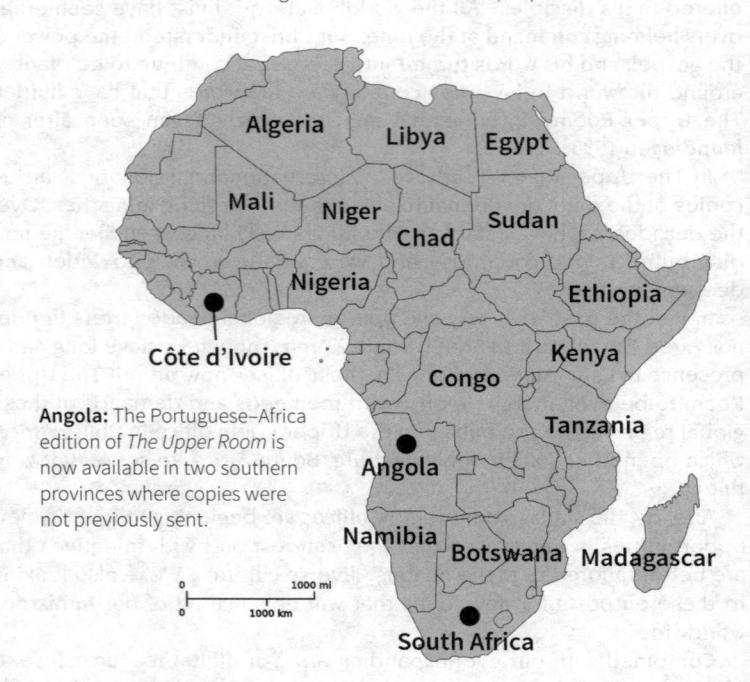

Angola: The Portuguese–Africa edition of *The Upper Room* is now available in two southern provinces where copies were not previously sent.

South Africa: Leslie Arendse, a retired electrician, has distributed *The Upper Room* for the past five years to police stations near his home. Copies are sent as far as 400 miles east, where a group eagerly awaits each issue of the Africa–English edition. 'These are not just stories. The devotions speak to each individual in a very special way,' Leslie says. 'Readers feel they are not alone.' Passionate about this ministry, he hopes someone younger will assume leadership one day.

The Editor writes...

At this time of year you might, like me, wonder what another new year has in store. You may even think up some new year resolutions: this will be the year when we finally lose weight, spend less time watching TV, do more exercise... we have a whole clean page of a brand new year ahead of us to fill with doing the right things, and there is no lack of advice as to how we should eat, drink and generally take care of ourselves.

I wonder how many of us stick to resolutions past the end of January. If we take on too many improving things there is a lot of discipline required and maybe too much of it all at once.

One thing I do try to be disciplined about, and not just in January, is to make some time each day to read my Bible and try to understand what God is saying to me through it. Our lives don't always allow for this at the same time every day: in the mornings we are up and off to work, or perhaps getting children ready for school; in the evenings we probably have meals to prepare, family commitments, church meetings or other social groups to attend. Life has never been busier and we find ourselves rushing from one appointment to another. Even our church lives can become so full that we can hardly find time for a quiet moment.

I have found that neglecting a quiet time, at some point in the day, can lead to a dry spiritual life. It is easy to leave God out of our priorities, but gradually the awareness of his presence with us, and the joy that we once knew from worship and prayer, disappears. Life itself can somehow seem grey and less vibrant.

Will you pledge, this January, to spend part of every day of this year with God? Think of what we could all learn from him by the time we reach another New Year's Eve!

Susan Hibbins
Editor of the UK edition

The Bible readings are selected with great care, and we urge you to include the suggested reading in your devotional time.

SUNDAY 1 JANUARY

What Time Is It?

Read Matthew 24:32–44

Teach us to count our days that we may gain a wise heart.
Psalm 90:12 (NRSV)

A new year makes me acutely conscious of the passage of time: how we allow calendars and clocks to dominate us, how there is never enough time for what we need or want to do. It reminds me how time changes some things but not others. Time helps to heal grief and softens memories of old conflicts and wounds, but the mere passage of time does not strengthen marriage, friendship or character.

A new year reminds us that God's time is different from ours. Galatians 4:4 says, 'when the fullness of time had come, God sent his Son' but we do not know God's future timetable. Some people try to predict the world's end or say we are living in 'end times', but in today's reading Jesus reminds us that only God knows what the future holds.

The best new year's resolution I can make is to appreciate each day God gives me, to become a better steward of my time, and to grow to be more Christ-like, the better to serve God.

Prayer: *Eternal God, teach us to use our days to 'gain a wise heart'. Amen*

Thought for the day: How will I resolve to serve God this year?

Gus Browning (Texas, US)

PRAYER FOCUS: TO BE A BETTER STEWARD OF MY TIME

MONDAY 2 JANUARY

Climbing Out of the Pit

Read 1 Thessalonians 5:16–18

In every thing give thanks: for this is the will of God in Christ Jesus concerning you.
1 Thessalonians 5:18 (KJV)

When I was a teenager, my brother and my father died within a few weeks of each other. Though the sun shone brightly that summer, my soul felt dark. Within 29 days, our family had been reduced from seven to five. Two chairs at the dinner table sat empty. Hopelessness trapped me in a deep hole.

Since I wasn't familiar with scripture, I stumbled in darkness for years, trying to climb out of my pit of despair. Then one day, I learned that Paul wrote, 'In every thing give thanks: for this is the will of God in Christ Jesus concerning you' (1 Thessalonians 5:18). I knew that God wanted me to be at peace, but I wondered how I could give thanks for tragedy and hopelessness. Then I scrutinised the verse, as if looking through a magnifying glass. A truth suddenly loomed large. Paul's letter to the Thessalonians does not command me to feel thankful or to be thankful; I must simply 'give thanks'.

God asks that we give thanks as an act of faith and obedience. We can learn to trust that he will walk with us through whatever lies ahead. If we feel ourselves slipping into a pit of sorrow, we can trust that he will hold us up.

Prayer: *Dear God, even in despair, help us to give thanks that you walk with us. Amen*

Thought for the day: God walks with me.

Mary Fran Heitzman (Minnesota, US)

PRAYER FOCUS: SOMEONE STRUGGLING WITH DEPRESSION

TUESDAY 3 JANUARY

Like a Tree

Read Psalm 1:1–3 and Jeremiah 17:7–8

Jesus said, 'Whoever drinks the water I give them will never thirst. Indeed, the water I give them will become in them a spring of water welling up to eternal life.'
John 4:14 (NIV)

The trees on the riverbank across from my house are not particularly beautiful, but they are sturdy and productive. A wide variety of birds finds refuge in their branches. People walking along the path by the river often stop and sit in the shade they provide. The pine cones they drop are collected by others as fuel for their fires.

During a recent drought the trees continued to flourish as their roots are deep, and they were nourished by the river. This reminded me that my life flourishes when I am rooted in the wisdom and truth of God's word, when I stay near the living water Jesus offers. By staying close to God, meditating on scripture and resting in God's presence, I can become spiritually strong. Then other parts of my life also move within the pattern God has set. When I overlook these spiritual disciplines, my life becomes less productive and I lose the peace and joy that God wants to give me. At such times I look at those trees and remember what my priorities need to be—keeping my life grounded in God's word and drinking the water Christ offers for eternal life.

Prayer: *Loving God, open our eyes to see and help us to learn the lessons your creation can teach us. Amen*

Thought for the day: My life flourishes when I rest in God's presence.

Ann Stewart (South Australia, Australia)

PRAYER FOCUS: ENVIRONMENTALISTS

WEDNESDAY 4 JANUARY

Patient Fishing

Read Matthew 4:18–22

'Come, follow me,' [Jesus] said, 'and I'll show you how to fish for people.'
Matthew 4:19 (CEB)

On a warm, tranquil evening last summer, a friend taught me to fish. He provided the equipment and instructed me on fish behaviour and bait. He emphasised the need for patience, especially when a fish is on the line and starts to fight. We rowed around the lake to his favourite fishing spots. But when I finally hooked a 'big one', I became overly aggressive and the line broke.

After this experience, the analogy between fishing for fish and fishing for people in today's reading became crystal clear to me. Opportunities to share our faith present themselves in daily life, often unexpectedly. The keys to success are knowledge, patience and—most importantly—being willing to go 'fishing'. While many get away, a few are hooked and those who get away remain for others to catch. We're not all equally equipped with the knowledge, patience and courage to catch everyone we witness to, but we can do our best in every human encounter, knowing that God will finish the work. Looking back on my faith journey, I am eternally grateful for the numerous brave people who relentlessly fished and prayed for me until I was finally hooked on God's eternal truths.

Prayer: *Dear God, show us how to tell our stories bravely and patiently, trusting you with the outcome. Amen*

Thought for the day: How will I follow Jesus' call to 'fish for people'?

Evan Wride (California, US)

PRAYER FOCUS: FOR PATIENCE IN SHARING MY FAITH

THURSDAY 5 JANUARY

Dancing for Joy

Read Psalm 34:1–7

The psalmist wrote, 'I will bless the Lord at all times; his praise shall continually be in my mouth.'
Psalm 34:1 (NRSV)

One grey London evening, I listened to a musician play in a public square. All around, toes tapped and fingers snapped in rhythm. Onlookers swayed, appearing tempted to dance; but nobody did, perhaps not wanting to look foolish in front of so many strangers. Then one man bent over, grabbed his little girl's hands and began to dance with her. The little girl swayed and stepped, not intimidated by the crowd. Eyes fixed on her father, she danced freely, and their joy in each other brightened the chilly dusk.

Often, like the onlookers in the crowd, I hold back from expressing my joy. I'm too afraid of people's opinions. Worshipping wholeheartedly is easy when everyone else is doing the same. But Psalm 34:1 says, 'I will bless the Lord at all times.'

Like the little girl dancing with her father, we can focus on God instead of the people around us and be free to worship him at any time. Today, let us praise God wholeheartedly.

Prayer: *Dear God, we want to worship you wholly, freely and joyfully. Please help us to keep our eyes on you and praise you as we pray, 'Father, hallowed be your name, your kingdom come. Give us each day our daily bread. Forgive us our sins, for we also forgive everyone who sins against us. And lead us not into temptation.'* Amen*

Thought for the day: I will praise the Lord no matter who is watching me.

Elizabeth Syson (Arizona, US)

PRAYER FOCUS: FATHERS AND DAUGHTERS
* Luke 11:2–4, NIV

FRIDAY 6 JANUARY

Quiet Transformation

Read John 2:1–11

We all, who with unveiled faces contemplate the Lord's glory, are being transformed into his image with ever-increasing glory, which comes from the Lord, who is the Spirit.
2 Corinthians 3:18 (NIV)

Jesus' first miracle began with ordinary water poured into commonplace stone jars. As far as we know, Jesus didn't stir the water, touch the jars or pray aloud. He simply asked the workers to serve the water to the wedding host. Obediently serving the host, they discovered that the water had been transformed into wine.

The Gospel author tells us that by this miracle, Jesus 'revealed his glory' (John 2:11) to his watching disciples. What did the disciples see that was so glorious? They saw that in Christ's powerful presence, transformation happens. Ordinary water becomes extraordinary wine as willing servants do what Jesus asks.

A similar quiet miracle of transformation happens in our lives. When we seek the presence of Christ, through meditation on scripture and through prayer, the Holy Spirit changes us gradually into our Lord's likeness. As we pour ourselves out in obedient service, we can become more and more like Jesus. Our ordinary lives can become extraordinary.

Prayer: *Lord Jesus, thank you for the ongoing miracle of transformation in our lives. Amen*

Thought for the day: Jesus Christ can change ordinary into extraordinary.

Marion Speicher Brown (Florida, US)

PRAYER FOCUS: NEWLYWEDS

SATURDAY 7 JANUARY

Wonderful, Isn't It?

Read Psalm 46:1-11
Who is it that conquers the world but the one who believes that Jesus is the Son of God?
1 John 5:5 (NRSV)

My father always sought to show us real-life stories of how God acts in our lives. One of those stories occurred in 1962, after the beginning of Angola's liberation struggle, when we were forced to take refuge in the woods far from our fields. One day my father and my cousin Martha were looking for food on the banks of the Dande River. While attempting to return to the other side—already loaded with goods and walking on one of the bridges made of two logs—my father slipped and fell. He was immediately swept away by the strong current of the waters. Since he did not know how to swim, he fought desperately for his life. When he became exhausted, he thought, 'Lord, thy will be done' (Matthew 6:10; 26:42). The waters carried him away. Suddenly, he felt something solid beneath him. Reinvigorated, he realised that he had been washed onto a large rock at the side of the turbulent river.

What a wonderful example of how we can all relinquish control of our lives to God's unending care! This story reminds me of times I have struggled to solve problems on my own. The solution may unexpectedly appear when I'm finally able to let go and turn the problem over to God.

Prayer: *Dear God, in times of distress, help us to remember that our salvation is in you. In Jesus' name. Amen*

Thought for the day: 'What is impossible for mortals is possible for God' (Luke 18:27).

Tito Bombo (Luanda, Angola)

PRAYER FOCUS: THOSE DISPLACED BY MILITARY CONFLICTS

SUNDAY 8 JANUARY

Hearts Full of Gratitude

Read John 6:5–13
When they had all had enough to eat, [Jesus] said to his disciples, 'Gather the pieces that are left over. Let nothing be wasted.'
John 6:12 (NIV)

I often make desk calendars with my church students as a way of welcoming the new year. Two years ago, however, after making our yearly desk calendar, I felt that throwing away the leftover paper would be wasteful. I put the scrap paper in my desk drawer for future use. Over the next two years, whenever I cleaned my desk, I wondered whether I should throw the paper away. The decision was never easy. The paper was high quality and came in a variety of pretty colours.

This year, while making cards of encouragement and consolation, I remembered the paper in my drawer. I used it to make several beautiful cards. Scripture reminds us of the importance of having the faith to receive God's gifts with thanksgiving. If we look on our surroundings with hearts full of gratitude, even old paper can become postcards that offer encouragement and strength.

Prayer: *Loving God, who created us with care, give us faith to see the beauty in all creation. We pray in Jesus' name. Amen*

Thought for the day: If we receive with thanks, we have nothing to throw away.

Eun-hye Cha (Seoul, South Korea)

PRAYER FOCUS: TO BE ABLE TO RECEIVE WITH THANKSGIVING

MONDAY 9 JANUARY

Wrestling with Doubt

Read Genesis 32:22–32

The man said, 'Your name will no longer be Jacob, but Israel, because you have struggled with God and with men and have overcome.'
Genesis 32:28 (NIV)

Sitting alone on a park bench, I fought back tears of frustration. I was certain that my life was dedicated to God and I tried to faithfully follow his leading. I had spent the past several years preparing for the career I believed God was calling me to, yet I couldn't even secure an interview. Had I so completely misunderstood God's direction, or had he simply given up on me? Throughout that night I struggled, wrestling with what my situation implied about my relationship with God.

Jacob, too, spent a night wrestling with God. Although the Bible doesn't say, I suspect that Jacob also worried about his relationship with God. Jacob had achieved great wealth by cheating his brother out of his rightful inheritance. Now, on the eve of their reunion, Jacob feared how Esau would receive him. However, at sunrise, in response to Jacob's request for blessing, the angel promised: 'Your name will… be… Israel, because you have struggled… and overcome' (Genesis 32:28).

Jacob's circumstances remained unchanged; his brother was still coming to meet him. But Jacob was a changed man. After my night of wrestling with God, my situation had not changed either. But I too had been changed; I was reassured that God wasn't offended by my doubts and would continue to love me unconditionally.

Prayer: *Heavenly Father, thank you for listening to our doubts and fears and for reassuring us of your unconditional love. Amen*

Thought for the day: Sometimes our failures provide the greatest opportunities to grow in faith.

Tom Dury (Colorado, US)

PRAYER FOCUS: SOMEONE SEARCHING FOR A JOB

TUESDAY 10 JANUARY

Still Working

Read Mark 9:38–41

Jesus replied [to John], 'Don't stop him. No one who does powerful acts in my name can quickly turn around and curse me. Whoever isn't against us is for us.'
Mark 9: 39–40 (CEB)

In today's reading, Jesus teaches his disciples to encourage genuine faith. John was troubled that another man was casting out demons even though he was not one of the twelve disciples. Jesus responded by teaching us all not to reject others because they don't belong to our group. We are all still working on our faith, still learning, still moving toward the same destination.

John's response to the man is a familiar one for many Christians. When we find a difference in practice, tradition or even music, we may discount all of the good work being accomplished by others. So often our divisions are caused by generational differences or human frailties rather than theological conflicts.

Today's story can help us to remember that if the gospel is being preached and the name of Jesus is being spoken, someone who needs to hear it will be reached. We may disagree amongst ourselves about the way the message is being delivered, where it is being taught or who is sharing it. But we know that Jesus can use anyone to reach the hearts of humanity.

Prayer: *Dear God, help us to look beyond our differences to focus on sharing your love with others. Amen*

Thought for the day: The good news of Christ can reach the world in many different ways.

Cheryl Anderson (California, US)

PRAYER FOCUS: CONGREGATIONS EXPERIENCING CONFLICT

WEDNESDAY 11 JANUARY

Expressions of Prayer

Read Philippians 4:4–9
In every situation, by prayer and petition, with thanksgiving, present your requests to God.
Philippians 4:6 (NIV)

I work as a hospital chaplain, providing spiritual and emotional care to patients and their families. Usually I end my visits by offering to pray with the patient, lifting to God the hopes, concerns, requests and joys they have named. But some patients aren't interested in deep conversation and simply want me to offer a prayer. I often feel that my prayers are shallow when I don't know what a patient holds dear in life, what their dreams and fears are and where they have invested their love.

When I shared this struggle with my supervisor, he responded by saying, 'You feel that these prayers are inadequate, because words are inadequate.' He is right. Even when I am able to craft and personalise my prayers carefully for a patient, words cannot adequately express the pain of parents who have lost a child, the joy of a new transplant recipient or the shock of a cancer patient given three months to live. 'Go and use words to pray with those families,' my supervisor continued. 'But remember that your presence, your body language and your ability to empathise are also a part of prayer.'

Maybe this is what Paul meant when he advised the Philippians to pray 'in every situation'. A rejoicing spirit, a gentle demeanour and a calm presence are powerful expressions of prayer.

Prayer: *O God, may our prayers extend beyond our words into our loving presence in the world. Amen*

Thought for the day: My prayers are meaningful even when words fail.

Teresa Coda (Massachusetts, US)

THURSDAY 12 JANUARY

Power of Silence

Read 1 Kings 19:9–18
There was a great wind… but the Lord was not in the wind; and after the wind an earthquake, but the Lord was not in the earthquake; and after the earthquake a fire, but the Lord was not in the fire; and after the fire a sound of sheer silence.
1 Kings 19:11–12 (NSRV)

I am an archaeologist and help to monitor construction activity at historic sites. Once, I was overseeing excavations near the city centre. It was noon. Work halted across the busy construction site for lunch. Mighty rock-chewing machines rattled to a halt and silence fell. Because my ears had grown accustomed to the pounding of jackhammers, the silence seemed strange. But it opened my ears to sounds previously unheard: vehicles braking at traffic lights, the car horn of an impatient driver, the city humming in the background. Then I heard a single church bell ringing in the distance. I wondered how many generations that bell had beckoned. How many people have been reminded of God by its tolling?

Then I realised that the silence allowed me to hear that bell. In this cacophonous world, we desperately need silence in order to hear God calling as Elijah did, 'Go out and stand on the mountain before the Lord, for the Lord is about to pass by' (1 Kings 19:11).

When we are afraid, we too might look for a hiding place. But if we listen—in silence—we will hear God calling us out of our fear into new paths of service.

Prayer: *O God, quiet our hearts and minds so that we may hear your voice and go where you send us. Amen*

Thought for the day: Silence allows me to hear God's voice.

Stephen Smith (Texas, US)

PRAYER FOCUS: THOSE AFRAID OF SILENCE

FRIDAY 13 JANUARY

In God's Own Time

Read Isaiah 40:28–31
Take delight in the Lord, and he will give you the desires of your heart.
Psalm 37:4 (NIV)

A friend gave me a pretty arrangement of flowers in various shades of orange. The greenery surrounding the flowers set off the vibrancy of their colours perfectly. However, the arrangement also contained the buds of three large lilies, and I found myself waiting impatiently for them to unfold and complete the effect. But the petals stayed firmly closed for several days. Then the first of the lilies bloomed. It was worth the wait; they added an extra glow and vitality to the arrangement at a time when I could have expected it to fade.

This made me think of how often we may become impatient and want all God's plans for us to unfold now. And then I realised that if the lilies had been flowering when I first received the arrangement, I probably would have taken them for granted. Their beauty was all the more precious to me because I had waited for them to bloom. Sometimes God is waiting for the right moment to bless us until we are fully ready to accept and appreciate the gift prepared for us.

Prayer: *Loving God, give us patience to appreciate all that you are and all the gifts that you pour out on us. Amen*

Thought for the day: God's gifts are worth waiting for.

Meg Mangan (New South Wales, Australia)

PRAYER FOCUS: THOSE IMPATIENT WITH GOD

SATURDAY 14 JANUARY

Guide My Journey

Read Psalm 119:105–112

[Wisdom cries out,] 'I love those who love me, and those who seek me find me.'
Proverbs 8:17 (NIV)

My family enjoys days out. As I plan each one, my goal is to determine the best route and clear directions. My car is equipped with technology that provides these answers. However, sometimes I still get lost because I have avoided or was careless in using this technology. My role is to 'ask' using my destination's address. The technology responds, 'Your route has been calculated.'

As I proceed, the technology gives me turn-by-turn directions, finally concluding with, 'You have arrived.' The technology is able to identify and respond to me uniquely, even though at the same time countless other people in countless other cars are asking similar questions. Noticing this, a family member once exclaimed, 'This must be how God hears and responds to all those prayers!'

Similarly, in my spiritual journey, I can ask God for guidance, discernment and direction. He is able to hear my requests in the midst of millions of other prayers offered at the same time. There are times when I haven't sought God, and I have gone in the wrong direction. But when we pray first, he can guide us through each day's challenges and temptations. Upon completion of our earthly journey, we can look forward to God's voice saying that we have arrived: 'Well done, good and faithful servant!' (Matthew 25:21).

Prayer: *Heavenly Father, help us seek the paths of righteousness each day. Amen*

Thought for the day: Each day I can ask and listen for God's guidance.

Doug Quinn (Oklahoma, US)

PRAYER FOCUS: THOSE WHO HAVE LOST THEIR WAY

SUNDAY 15 JANUARY

Reflected Light

Read 2 Corinthians 3:17–18
We all, who with unveiled faces contemplate the Lord's glory, are being transformed into his image with ever-increasing glory, which comes from the Lord, who is the Spirit.
2 Corinthians 3:18 (NIV)

I was walking down the lane near our house one raw winter's day. The branches of the trees were black against the slate grey sky. The fields were a dull brown in the low winter light. In front of me was a muddy, dirty rain puddle. Suddenly, in the puddle, I could see a reflection of the clouds which were at that moment illuminated by the setting sun: yellow, crimson, turquoise. That dirty, unremarkable strip of water was transformed into something of wonder. As I paused to look, the words quote above came into my mind.

I understood afresh how we Christians, like that dirty brown puddle, are being gradually changed into the people the Lord intends us to be. This transformation comes about in part, not by striving or huge effort on our part, but simply by turning our faces to the Lord and his light, so that we reflect his glory. The word 'contemplate' resonates with me. As we take time to be still in his presence, to meditate on his word and to let him speak to us through his creation, so we are gradually changed to be more like him. All the puddle did was to reflect the light shining onto it, and this is what God calls us to do too.

Prayer: *Help me, Lord, to take one or two moments today simply to rest in your presence, and to trust that you are transforming me as you have promised. Amen*

Thought for the day: We are being recreated in God's image.

Gillian Tetmar (Somerset, UK)

PRAYER FOCUS: THOSE WHO ARE SEEKING GOD'S LIGHT TODAY

MONDAY 16 JANUARY

Journals of Praise

Read Deuteronomy 11:18–20
Remember the wonders he has done, his miracles, and the judgements he pronounced.
1 Chronicles 16:12 (NIV)

Several years ago, I began to incorporate writing in a spiritual journal as part of my devotional time. I had always written my requests and the desires of my heart—my cries to Jesus—in blue ink. It seemed that I was always begging God for something.

One winter, as the new year approached, I felt the Lord prompt me to write about the things I am thankful for. I decided to write these in black ink and label them 'God's Blessings'. I was amazed to see how many blessings God bestows on me throughout the day. Some blessings are small. Some are much bigger miracles.

I have become so much more aware of God's love and blessings in every moment of the day. I no longer overlook God's mercies or take them for granted. Now, when I flip through my devotional journal, my many blessings penned in black ink stand out. When we take note of God's blessings each day, we can experience his love more fully.

Prayer: *Dear Lord, help us to become more aware of the many ways you bless us each day. We pray as Jesus taught us, saying, 'Our Father in heaven, hallowed be your name, your kingdom come, your will be done, on earth as it is in heaven. Give us today our daily bread. And forgive us our debts, as we also have forgiven our debtors. And lead us not into temptation, but deliver us from the evil one.'* Amen*

Thought for the day: How can I be aware of God's blessings today?

Rebecca Seaton (Tennessee, US)

PRAYER FOCUS: GRATITUDE FOR GOD'S BLESSINGS
* Matthew 6:9–13, NIV

TUESDAY 17 JANUARY

Miracles Happen

Read John 16:22–24
We know that all things work together for good for those who love God, who are called according to his purpose.
Romans 8:28 (NRSV)

My six-year-old son, Sabalo, had been diagnosed with a tumour. After many medical examinations, including two biopsies, we learned that the tumour was growing and could not be successfully treated by radiation.

Five years after the diagnosis, Sabalo's difficulties with mobility had increased. His spine showed a severe deviation. He could not sit down comfortably and spent most of his time lying in bed. Going to school was a major effort. When Sabalo woke up feeling ill, he said to me, 'I do not want to grow up like this.' Still we trusted in God, and we did not lose faith.

We experienced a miracle in June 2006. The director of the oncology centre transferred Sabalo to a surgeon who understood the boy's suffering, had compassion on him, and assumed the risks of performing an operation to remove the mass. The operation was successful and cost us nothing. In a world in which love for neighbours sometimes seems hard to find, this doctor's compassion renewed my faith that 'all things work together for good for those who love God'.

Prayer: *Thank you, Lord, for leading us in the way of compassion. Amen*

Thought for the day: 'All things are possible for God' (Matthew 19:26, CEB).

Arnaldo K. Ingo (Luanda, Angola)

PRAYER FOCUS: CHILDREN UNDERGOING SURGERY

WEDNESDAY 18 JANUARY

Not Giving Up

Read 1 Thessalonians 4:1–2
Brothers and sisters, we instructed you how to live in order to please God, as in fact you are living. Now we ask you and urge you in the Lord Jesus to do this more and more.
1 Thessalonians 4:1 (NIV)

Some months ago I joined my local church's prayer shawl ministry and began knitting and crocheting with a group of women. In the early stages of my work with the group, my first few rows would go well, but then I would drop stitches and end up with an uneven piece. As frustrating as it was, I had to undo my work and start again. In time, with practice and focus, I am becoming more skilled.

Following Jesus can be like my experiences with knitting and crocheting. As we seek to grow in our relationship with God, we deal with challenges and we do not always get it right. This is nothing new for Christians. In today's verse, the apostle Paul encouraged the believers to continue to increase their faith in God, despite the challenges they faced. The Christian journey requires persistence. We do not always get it right but we cannot give up.

I am now in my fifth month with the prayer shawl ministry. This new calling has proved to be very fulfilling. I meet new people with whom I share many things. Though I still drop stitches and sometimes have to start again, I produce beautiful pieces that help me minister to individuals I have never met. My faith journey and this ministry are ongoing, and I am not giving up.

Prayer: *Dear God, give us the strength to continue serving you even when we don't get it right the first time. Amen*

Thought for the day: Being faithful to God requires persistence.

Claudine Glasgow-Brooks (Tennessee, US)

PRAYER FOCUS: MEMBERS OF HEALING MINISTRIES

THURSDAY 19 JANUARY

Broken

Read Ephesians 4:25–32
If you remember that your brother or sister has something against you, leave your gift… before the altar and go; first be reconciled to your brother or sister, and then come and offer your gift.
Matthew 5:23–24 (NRSV)

When an item breaks, I have three responses: (1) I'm unhappy; (2) I'm frustrated; (3) I'm challenged to mend it. The first two responses rarely last long. In a short time, I am ready to find some tools and fix the problem. I love to take things apart to see how they work or how they can be repaired.

However, mending objects is easier than mending relationships. At times, I have wounded others with my harsh words or a mean spirit. In those moments, I wish I could run to the toolbox for a wrench, screwdriver or pliers. But a wrench or screwdriver can't reduce the pain I have caused. And words alone are not sufficient to take away another's anguish, even if I meant no harm.

When we have hurt someone with our words, we can turn to God's word, which reminds us that repentance and forgiveness are needed. When we sincerely repent, God helps us through our troubles—even those we have caused ourselves. God instructs us in ways of reconciliation (Matthew 5:23–24) and reminds us to be patient (Psalm 40:1–3). Repairing broken relationships is not easy, but knowing God's promises and seeing them fulfilled in the lives of his people in the Bible gives us hope. Our relationships can be restored because through it all, God will stand by us and guide us.

Prayer: *Dear God, lead us to speak words of kindness and truth as we seek forgiveness and restoration. Amen*

Thought for the day: God wants a deeper relationship with us.

Gary A. Miller (California, US)

PRAYER FOCUS: THOSE SEEKING GOD'S FORGIVENESS

FRIDAY 20 JANUARY

The Benefit of the Present

Read Ecclesiastes 7:13–18
When times are good, be happy; but when times are bad, consider this: God has made the one as well as the other. Therefore, no one can discover anything about their future.
Ecclesiastes 7:14 (NIV)

On a Friday afternoon, I was driving along the motorway outside Washington, DC, when I came upon a flashing alert sign that read: 'Traffic ahead next 2 miles'. I thought, 'Really? You have to tell me that? It's a Friday afternoon on the motorway. Of course there's traffic!' The next message on the sign appeared: 'Watch for stopped…'. Now it made sense. The entire message couldn't be displayed on one sign, so the two halves alternated; I had read the second half of the message first. I thought how funny that was. Even if God were to show us our future, it wouldn't make sense to us without the benefit of the present. It would be like getting the second half of the message first.

I thought of Ecclesiastes 7:14. I have always struggled with wanting to know how situations are going to work out, especially when I'm going through a difficult time. But God made it clear to me: even if he were to show us what the future holds, the future wouldn't make sense to us until we had experienced today, the present, leading up to it. When we are worried or anxious about the future, we can remember God's promise to be with us always.

Prayer: *Dear God, give us peace and joy today, even if we are uncertain about the future. Amen*

Thought for the day: I cannot add days to my life through worrying (see Matthew 6:27).

Sheyanne Armstrong (Virginia, US)

PRAYER FOCUS: COMMUTERS

SATURDAY 21 JANUARY

Storms of Life

Read Psalm 55:4–8

Cast your cares on the Lord and he will sustain you; he will never let the righteous be shaken.
Psalm 55:22 (NIV)

The day was stormy. Lightning flashed all around. The wind howled, the rain fell and tornadoes threatened. At the radio station in Athens, Georgia, where I worked while I was at college, the owner of the station concluded his morning broadcast as usual with, 'It's a lovely day to be in Athens.' Afterward, I met him in the hallway and kidded him about the current state of the weather. I asked, 'How can today be a lovely day to be in Athens?' He put his arm around my shoulder and said, 'During World War II, I was a bomber pilot. Early in the war, my plane was shot down; and I spent the rest of my time in a prisoner-of-war camp. After that ordeal, I promised that if I made it home, I would not let anything ruin my day. Every day I'm here is a lovely day to be in Athens.'

I have thought about his words often over the years. I realised that as we face the storms in our lives, we tend to lose sight of the comfort we know simply by living in God's love. Too often we forget about the blessings, mercy, grace and love of God, and we focus on whatever storm is at hand. We forget to put our trust in the Lord. Today, when facing the storms of life, I remember the words of the radio station owner, and I am thankful that God is present to calm the raging storms of life.

Prayer: *Dear Lord, thank you for looking after us and loving us during the storms of life. Amen*

Thought for the day: Storms come and go, but God's love is unchanging.

Larry Wayne (Tennessee, US)

PRAYER FOCUS: RADIO BROADCASTERS

SUNDAY 22 JANUARY

Seeing the Potential

Read 1 Samuel 16:1–13

Do not judge, so that you may not be judged.
Matthew 7:1 (NRSV)

The plant had only two puny leaves sticking out of a dirty clay pot. When one of the rummage-sale workers asked me, 'Will you take it?' my first thought was, 'Another plant? That scrawny thing?' But then I remembered a small space on my kitchen windowsill, just the right size for the ugly pot, and I brought it home. If this plant were to die, nothing would be lost. As the months passed, one more leaf and then another and another appeared. With warm sunshine and an occasional drink of water, the little plant began to thrive.

Every time I look at the now-flourishing plant, I am reminded of how easily I make judgements about the potential of everything from plants to people. I think, 'Oh, she'll never amount to anything; look at all her tattoos!' or 'What chance does he have, coming from a home like that?' or 'She shouldn't employ him; he's done time in prison.'

God looks at people's hearts, not their outward appearance or circumstances. Jesus reminds us in Matthew 7:1 not to condemn people. Instead, we can help others experience God's love, care and grace—and then step back and watch for the transformations.

Prayer: *O Lord, help us today to refrain from judging others and instead to see each person as someone of worth, created in your image. Amen*

Thought for the day: Today, I will try to see others through God's eyes.

Nancy Clark (Michigan, US)

PRAYER FOCUS: SOMEONE I HAVE JUDGED

MONDAY 23 JANUARY

God Is Near

Read Genesis 28:15–16

'Am I only a God nearby,' declares the Lord, 'and not a God far away? Who can hide in secret places so that I cannot see them?' declares the Lord. 'Do not I fill heaven and earth?' declares the Lord.
Jeremiah 23:23–24 (NIV)

Significant life changes can cause us to feel confused or lost. When familiar things are replaced by the unfamiliar, God can seem distant and unconcerned. That was how I felt after moving to the bustling metropolis of Istanbul, a city of more than 15 million people.

My wife, our two children and I had moved into a small apartment in a crowded part of the city. It was at the crossroads of two busy streets. The traffic noise was unlike anything I had ever experienced, and it seemed to be constant throughout the day and night. The Muslim call to prayer rang out from several different mosques in our neighbourhood. I was thousands of miles away from the spacious house I had been living in for the past seven years. Confronted with unfamiliar surroundings, I began to wonder, 'Lord, did I hear you correctly? Are you really with me in this move?'

Then I remembered what God asked in Jeremiah 23:24: 'Do not I fill heaven and earth?' I realised that God was encouraging me to trust in him, the one who is always steadfast, even as I dealt with so much uncertainty. I could never escape God's care, even in this faraway and unfamiliar place. In fact, during the months that followed, God's presence became more real to me than it would have been if I had chosen to stay in my comfortable surroundings.

Prayer: *Dear Lord, in lonely and uncomfortable surroundings, may we turn to you, our constant companion and ever present help. Amen*

Thought for the day: God is nearby—even in faraway places.

Timothy Austin (Turkey)

PRAYER FOCUS: THOSE FACING CHANGE

TUESDAY 24 JANUARY

Calling All Volunteers!

Read Exodus 35:4–9

I heard the voice of the Lord saying, 'Whom shall I send? And who will go for us?' And I said, 'Here am I. Send me!"
Isaiah 6:8 (NIV)

This verse from Isaiah was one of the verses that touched my mother's heart with the desire to become a missionary. Many times I heard the story of how my mum felt called as a young girl to go and preach overseas. But she was from a very poor and uneducated family. In fact, she was the first person in her family to graduate from college. Nevertheless, she surrendered to God's call, went to nursing school and there met a young medical student who also felt called to missionary service.

Even though this verse is quite familiar to me, last Sunday I gained new insight into its meaning: God takes volunteers! Whether a person is rich or poor, educated or uneducated, God openly receives all who volunteer to be of service. He has work that can be done by anyone and everyone.

In today's reading Moses tells the children of Israel that everyone who is willing should bring the Lord an offering for a special purpose: 'Everyone who is willing' (Exodus 35:5). Isn't that wonderful? God takes volunteers and gives them amazing jobs to do!

Prayer: *Gracious heavenly Father, give us willing hearts to serve you. In your Son's name. Amen*

Thought for the day: If I volunteer, God will give me work to do.

Harriet Michael (Kentucky, US)

PRAYER FOCUS: FOR THE SPIRIT TO SERVE

WEDNESDAY 25 JANUARY

Soul Answers

Read Romans 8:18–39

The steadfast love of the Lord never ceases, his mercies never come to an end; they are new every morning; great is your faithfulness.
Lamentations 3:22–23 (NRSV)

'Why?' I sobbed into my husband's arms. A joyous occasion had turned to despair. After a 24-hour labour, our baby boy was dead.

Fifty years later, I still remember the chill of the hospital room, the nurse's frantic voice and the doctor's words. 'I'm sorry; the baby didn't make it.' I could not grasp his words. The threads of my mind were tangled. For days, months and years, I was desperate to resolve my loss. Did I do something wrong? Did the doctor? Did God? How could a loving God have allowed this?

Sadness overwhelmed me. The birth of friends' babies brought me tears instead of joy. Seeing baby clothes in the shops saddened me. Children reminded me of that dreaded day. I continued to mourn the past and to persist in asking questions, though no answers could satisfy my mind. Only prayer and scripture brought answers to my soul: deep, unspoken answers that gave me joy in the midst of sorrow. God's loving-kindness and compassion sustained me. The memories still bring a tear, but I trust that in divine wisdom, God takes the good and bad in our lives, untangles them and brings new beginnings.

Prayer: *Dear Lord, lead us through our grief. Help us to see your light and to remember your love. Amen*

Thought for the day: Prayer and scripture reading can sustain me in times of sorrow.

Pamela J. Caldwell (California, US)

PRAYER FOCUS: THOSE WHO HAVE LOST A CHILD

THURSDAY 26 JANUARY

The Importance of Recharging

Read John 12:20–33
Jesus said, 'Now my soul is troubled.'
John 12:27 (NRSV)

A friend of mine was showing me the features of his new smartphone. Suddenly, a shrill beeping assaulted our ears and he read a notification. Then we heard a low humming noise and the screen went black. 'The battery is dead and I don't have the charger with me,' he said with disappointment. Even with all its capabilities, the most important item of equipment needed was a simple battery recharger.

In the scripture above Jesus described himself as troubled; but he was aware of the purpose of this hour and the sacrifice he would make for all of humanity. God proclaimed to all that Jesus would be glorified. A troubled Jesus and those present needed God's words at that moment. They needed strength.

Sometimes, like my friend's phone, we need to be recharged. Even the strongest of saints needs encouragement. We get caught up in life's challenges and stress. Our souls become troubled. That's when we can turn to God for encouragement and strength. Perhaps God speaks to us through a kind word from a friend, or— through prayer and Bible study—he recharges our hearts. When life feels very draining and the next step is a mystery, we can seek the recharging power of a God who loves us so very much.

Prayer: *Dear God, remind us to look to you to be revitalised. Amen*

Thought for the day: When life depletes us, God can recharge our spirits.

Steve Burns (Arkansas, US)

PRAYER FOCUS: THOSE SEEKING REFRESHMENT

FRIDAY 27 JANUARY

Looking for the Beauty

Read Matthew 25:31–40

'The King will reply, "Truly I tell you, whatever you did for one of the least of these brothers and sisters of mine, you did for me."'
Matthew 25:40 (NIV)

At the beginning of our trip to Western Australia, I was looking forward to seeing wildflowers. As we drove around, I scanned the edges of the roadside where I'd seen them on a previous visit. But because we were travelling earlier in the season and after a period of insufficient rainfall, many of the plants had not blossomed.

Then a regular traveller told us, 'Look in the gravel heaps off the road. You need to go farther in; you can't always see them from the road.' We took her advice and found wildflowers in the most unlikely places. We discovered them among rocks and gravel—tiny flowers in crevices, their beauty brightening up the sometimes-barren landscape. We never expected to find such beauty in places so hot and dry.

In a similar way, sometimes we don't see the beauty of people when we first encounter them. But when we take time to look deeper, we can find the worth in every person. Wherever he travelled, Jesus often associated with the outcasts of society, the unloved, those considered unclean, and he calls us to do the same.

Prayer: *Loving God, help us take the time to see the beauty you see in others. In the name of Jesus we pray. Amen*

Thought for the day: Today I will show God's love to someone who seems unlovable.

Lenore Warton (New South Wales, Australia)

PRAYER FOCUS: TRAVELLERS

SATURDAY 28 JANUARY

Rest Practice

Read Matthew 11:28–30
Those who enter God's rest also cease from their labours as God did from his. Let us therefore make every effort to enter that rest.
Hebrews 4:10–11 (NRSV)

I sat at my drums, music playing through my headphones, my hands and feet moving in time to the song I was learning for a theatre production. My eyes tracked the music on the printed score. The song was fun to play—and so easy. Suddenly, all I heard was the out-of-place thud, thud, thud of my sticks hitting the drums. The music had stopped, but I had kept playing. I had ignored the rest sign that signalled me to stop.

I restarted the song and began again with my head nodding to the beat. My mind wandered just for a second, and once again I didn't stop at the rest. I knew such a mistake would ruin the performance, so the only answer was for me to practise resting. I played the song again and again, and after enough practice, I got it right!

When I finally turned off the music and set down my drumsticks, I realised that too often I miss the rests in my life. Too often I keep going in my own strength when I need to stop and remember God's desire for me to be quiet and still. I decided then that I would practise resting. By God's grace, we can learn to follow the rhythm he has established for each of us.

Prayer: *Dear Lord, help us to practise resting in your presence. Amen*

Thought for the day: Perfect rest in God requires practice.

Sherrie Lorance (California, US)

PRAYER FOCUS: MUSICIANS

SUNDAY 29 JANUARY

Fresh and Green

Read Psalm 92:6–15

The righteous will… still bear fruit in old age, they will stay fresh and green, proclaiming, 'The Lord is upright; he is my Rock, and there is no wickedness in him.'
Psalm 92:12, 14–15 (NIV)

Standing in Sequoia National Forest, among some of the oldest trees in the world, always makes me look up. I am amazed to be in the presence of something that old which is still growing, still alive. I felt the same awe when I walked on the Mount of Olives and saw trees that Jesus prayed beneath. How could anything that old remain living?

The last time I visited Sequoia, it suddenly occurred to me that even old things can reflect God's glory. That includes those of us who feel we have lived long past our prime, especially those who need help with daily tasks.

The sense of being old can bring a feeling of hopelessness. 'Why is God keeping me here?' I ask myself. 'Why doesn't God take me home?' And then I think of the trees. They are here to make us look up as they point heavenward. And God still works through those of us who are advanced in years. We may be old, but we are also a reminder that God cares and he loves us.

Prayer: *Dear God, thank you for the gift of long life. Help us to live our lives as a way of giving thanks to you. Amen*

Thought for the day: I am never too old to proclaim God's goodness and love.

Alvin E. Trucano (Nebraska, US)

PRAYER FOCUS: OLDER ADULTS

MONDAY 30 JANUARY

Treasure in the Heart

Read Matthew 6:19–21
Where your treasure is, there your heart will be also.
Matthew 6:21 (NRSV)

My daughter wanted to redecorate her room, which was full of souvenirs and childhood toys. As I helped her get rid of the clutter and decorate with new curtains and bedding, my spirit was lifted by such a clean and orderly room! Her desk now had room for flowers and a Bible, and I hoped that her eyes would be drawn to beauty and her heart drawn to God. A sense of well-being came over me.

Inspired, I tried to clean the rest of our home myself. I discovered that while it was easy for me to get rid of my daughter's possessions, it was much harder to get rid of mine! But my collection of keepsakes not only occupied physical space, they burdened my mind and weighed on my spirit. Similarly, social media and other activities can occupy my mind, leaving little room for me to store up spiritual things.

When we make room in our days for scripture reading and prayer, then our spirits can be strengthened with treasure from the Bible. God's wisdom and guidance will help us in our relationships and in our service to God and his people.

Prayer: *Dear God, help us to rid our lives of those things that draw us away from you. May we be filled with your word and the promptings of your Holy Spirit. Amen*

Thought for the day: When I clean out the clutter I make room for the Holy Spirit.

Frieda Yang (California, US)

PRAYER FOCUS: MOTHERS AND DAUGHTERS

TUESDAY 31 JANUARY

Taste and See

Read Psalm 34:8–14

Taste and see that the Lord is good; blessed is the one who takes refuge in him.
Psalm 34:8 (NIV)

When I asked about the growing popularity of alligator-tail cuisine, people often said, 'It tastes like chicken.' However, when I thought of an alligator, I could not imagine that any part of it would taste good, let alone 'like chicken'. However, when a trusted colleague ordered the exotic dish at a local restaurant, I decided to try it myself. It didn't taste like chicken, but it was a lot better than I had expected. When fried, it reminded me of shrimp; and in sausage, it was surprisingly flavourful and rich.

I realised that my feelings about this new food—apprehension, trial and joy—appear in my faith as well. The psalmists frequently wrote of the goodness, majesty, mercy, abundance and love of God, encouraging each of us to go beyond knowing about his glory, to 'taste and see' for ourselves that he is good.

Like tasting and trying a great new food, when we taste the goodness of God we find a love and grace that satisfies and nourishes. It can exceed our imagination and remind us of our heart's deepest longing. God is rich in goodness and in steadfast love.

Prayer: *Dear God, our hearts are desperate for truth, love, hope and joy. In you, we find all the goodness we seek. Thank you. Amen*

Thought for the day: God's grace can nourish and satisfy me.

Cassius Rhue (South Carolina, US)

WEDNESDAY 1 FEBRUARY

To Heal a Broken Heart

Read 1 Corinthians 13:1–13
I will show you the most excellent way.
1 Corinthians 12:31 (NIV)

We have an old beagle named Shorty. He wandered on to our land 17 years ago. He'd been abused, judging by the way he made a hasty retreat the moment any of us came close to him. Yet he became an instant friend to our dog, Ollie, and thus became a part of the family. It took him a long time, but bit by bit and pat by pat, he began to trust us.

Much has changed in the years since Shorty came our way. Now when anyone in the family calls his name, he comes running, long ears flopping and tail wagging. He rolls over for a pat, totally trusting his human family. Through lots of love, care and quiet gentleness, he learned that he could trust his big, wonderful family.

Every now and then, people a lot like Shorty come into our lives. They have been broken physically, mentally, emotionally and spiritually. Trusting anyone is nearly impossible for them. The family of God can begin the healing process for the broken-hearted. When we take the time to offer a safe place of love, trustworthiness and grace, we can be a part of the miracle of restoration and redemption.

Prayer: *Dear God, let us bring healing to those who are hurting, through your power and love in Christ Jesus. Amen*

Thought for the day: Who in my life needs to hear words of hope and grace?

B.J. Mathias (Mississippi, US)

PRAYER FOCUS: ANIMAL SHELTERS

THURSDAY 2 FEBRUARY

In God's Hands

Read Isaiah 49:8–16
With a strong hand and outstretched arm—God's faithful love lasts forever!
Psalm 136:12 (CEB)

Several years ago, my 13-year-old daughter needed back surgery to straighten her spine. The diagnosis terrified us. The curve in her back was extensive and she faced a long operation.

During the operation, my husband and I prayed with family and friends. About four hours into it, a friend came to the waiting room and handed us a small statue of two hands holding a praying angel. The statue was engraved, 'God is holding you in the palms of his hands.' I was immediately comforted. The image of God holding our daughter and us during the surgery was a powerful reminder that we are never alone in our fears and struggles. Our daughter's operation was a success and she is fine today. My little statue holds a prominent place in my living room and has remained for me an image of God's comfort.

I have returned many times to the image of being held in the hands of God. Throughout their history, the people of God suffered; but Isaiah reminded them that no matter what they were going through, God was holding them. We also have struggles and pain as we journey through life. We are reminded that God is not only with us; he holds us.

Prayer: *Holy God, remind us that you are always holding us in the palms of your hands. Amen*

Thought for the day: God tenderly holds me every day.

Patricia M. Daniels (Florida, US)

PRAYER FOCUS: SURGEONS

FRIDAY 3 FEBRUARY

Three to Thirty

Read Luke 16:1–13

Whoever is faithful in a very little is faithful also in much; and whoever is dishonest in a very little is dishonest also in much.
Luke 16:10 (NRSV)

A school headteacher approached our church about providing rucksacks filled with food items for a few local schools to send home each Friday with students who were unlikely to have much to eat at the weekend. After a few weeks, more schools contacted us. What began with three schools had grown to 30, seemingly overnight. Each time we said yes without hesitation, but we began to wonder if our small church could actually maintain the increase.

The congregation continued to donate money and food items to fill the rucksacks each week. No money from the church's budget went to this particular programme since the budget was already committed to other ministries. Amazingly, we always had enough to fill the rucksacks.

Through this ministry we saw scripture being fulfilled. Jesus said that those who are faithful in the little things will also be faithful in the big things, and scripture reassures us that God will provide. When we respond each time God calls us, we learn that a little faith can open the door to show his awesome power.

Prayer: *Dear Lord, help us to be faithful in all things, especially in the little things. Help us to have the faith that you will provide as we seek to minister to others. In Jesus' name we pray. Amen*

Thought for the day: God magnifies my faithful giving.

Andy Clapp (North Carolina, US)

PRAYER FOCUS: CHILDREN WITHOUT ENOUGH TO EAT

SATURDAY 4 FEBRUARY

New Purpose

Read Psalm 127:1–2
Unless the Lord builds the house, the builders labour in vain.
Psalm 127:1 (NIV)

We were on holiday in York, a beautiful, historic city in northern England, filled with overhanging Elizabethan buildings, Georgian and Victorian houses, medieval churches, city walls and Roman remains. During our stay, we observed workmen restoring an old building nearby. Workers came early each morning and set about unloading supplies required for the transformation of the old building into something new that would stand the test of time. With plenty of noisy crashing, they discarded rubble in a pile ready for removal.

Later, while praying and listening for God one morning, I remembered Psalm 127:1: 'Unless the Lord builds the house, the builders labour in vain.' I invited God to transform my life, regarding it as his temple to be restored, renewed and improved. Thinking of the builders, I was nervous that my inner change might be radical or painful; but I remembered that God always comes to us lovingly to restore us, to strengthen us and to give us new purpose.

Prayer: *Dear God, may we be open to the changes you make so that we can be more effective in your service. Amen*

Thought for the day: God can restore me and give me new purpose.

Faith Ford (Herefordshire, England)

PRAYER FOCUS: CONSTRUCTION WORKERS

SUNDAY 5 FEBRUARY

Listening to God or Goliath?

Read 1 Samuel 17:41–51
David said to the Philistine, 'You come against me with sword and spear and javelin, but I come against you in the name of the Lord Almighty, the God of the armies of Israel, whom you have defied.'
1 Samuel 17:45 (NIV)

When David fought Goliath, he had a choice. He could believe either the taunts of Goliath or the promises of God. Replying to the Philistine with today's verse, David chose God—and Goliath lost his head.

Every day, we have choices about what messages we will believe: those that come from the world around us or those from our God. When I feel as if the world is telling me, 'You're a loser, a worthless failure. No one loves you', God counters, 'You're my child and I love you unconditionally.' 'You're out of work and you're going to starve' say the words of doubt. But God says, 'I will provide for you.' When we hear, 'You have six months to live', Jesus reminds us: 'In me, you have eternal life.' When a voice within badgers us with, 'Your prodigal children are lost', God gives us hope: 'I can guide them home.'

Even when we feel completely alone, the words of Jesus remind us we are loved: 'Surely I am with you always' (Matthew 28:20). We have a choice. Which promises shall we believe: taunts that echo our doubts or promises that come from the love of God?

Prayer: *Dear Father, help us listen to your voice through scripture, other believers and your Spirit. Amen*

Thought for the day: I can trust in God's promises today and every day.

James N. Watkins (Indiana, US)

PRAYER FOCUS: SOMEONE STRUGGLING TO TRUST GOD'S LOVE

MONDAY 6 FEBRUARY

Walking With Me

Read Psalm 37:25–29

Our steps are made firm by the Lord, when he delights in our way; though we stumble, we shall not fall headlong, for the Lord holds us by the hand.
Psalm 37:23–24 (NRSV)

My husband and I are enjoying watching our eleven-month-old son, Adam, learn to walk. Every day, we take him by the hand, lift him up and guide him as he takes a few cautious steps. We are always careful to direct him toward a safe destination, making sure that he does not run into cabinets and sharp table corners. I remember that the first time Adam stumbled and fell he looked up at us as if to say, 'Why did you let me fall?' We simply smiled reassuringly at him and reached down to help him up. Then he happily continued to toddle as if nothing had happened.

For me, this experience is similar to the way our heavenly Father guides us. When something bad happens to me, I've often questioned, 'Father, why did you let me fall?' But every time, God reassures me. He is always there—stretching out a hand, waiting to lift me up to continue my journey. God never promised that we wouldn't face trials or even stumble at times, but he did promise never to stop guiding us. With that promise, we can continue to live in confidence as he directs us.

Prayer: *Dear Father, thank you for directing our steps, lifting us up when we fall and placing us back on the right path. Amen*

Thought for the day: With my hand in God's hand I may stumble, but I will never fall.

Latonika Blackmon (Tennessee, US)

PRAYER FOCUS: PARENTS OF TODDLERS

TUESDAY 7 FEBRUARY

Set Free

Read Luke 4:16–21

[Jesus] began by saying to them, 'Today this scripture is fulfilled in your hearing.'
Luke 4:21 (NIV)

Israel awaited a Messiah that they knew would one day come to liberate them. Jesus shocks the people in the synagogue saying, 'Today this scripture is fulfilled in your hearing.' In other words, 'Today is the day of your liberation.' Jesus' words are still true today; his task as Messiah is to set free all those who are captive.

In 2008 on a mission trip to Egypt, I met a young man who had recently attempted to commit suicide by jumping into the River Nile. A woman who saw his intention had cried out to him, 'Young man, you can jump and end this life, but what about the other one?' That woman's question stopped him from carrying out his plan. He decided instead to try to find God.

After hearing his story, I shared the gospel with him. With tears in his eyes, he accepted Christ. I hugged him, and he told me that no one had given him a hug in seven years. He experienced first-hand what it means to be set free. This could not have happened without his hearing the good news of the liberator, Jesus, who still sets us free today!

Prayer: *Lord Jesus, you have the power to set us free. Help us to find rest in your arms. Amen*

Thought for the day: Jesus can set me free.

Cristian Istrate (Sibiu, Romania)

PRAYER FOCUS: THOSE CONTEMPLATING SUICIDE

WEDNESDAY 8 FEBRUARY

Serving Quietly

Read Romans 12:4–8

We must help the weak, remembering the words the Lord Jesus himself said: 'It is more blessed to give than to receive.'
Acts 20:35 (NIV)

My husband, Bill, is naturally curious and observant, which contributes to his skill with his hands. He's never been afraid to try to fix anything. He fondly recalls, when he was young, working alongside 'Uncle' Walter, a family friend, on run-down cars in a nearby garage. Bill remembers testing, probing, adjusting and recalibrating engine parts, ball bearings, exhaust fans—you name it. He would observe Walter and then try his own hand at it.

Throughout our many years together, I've witnessed Bill's ability to build or repair just about anything, whether it's for a family member, a friend, or someone at work or church. It used to upset me that people would constantly ask him to fix things, sometimes even before a word of hello. But upon reflection one day, I saw his talent as his gift from God. That change in my perspective has made all the difference.

I wonder if I offer my own gifts cheerfully without thought or regard for myself. Will I someday mature so that I don't need or expect credit for my service to others? I see clearly that Bill is freely giving of himself for the sake of others, as God wants us to do. When we watch people like Bill, we can see examples of serving God quietly and strive to do likewise.

Prayer: *O God, inspire us to discover and use our talents in daily service to others and to do so with joy. Amen*

Thought for the day: My cheerful giving is a testament to God's grace.

Deborah Burke Henderson (Massachusetts, US)

PRAYER FOCUS: CAR MECHANICS

THURSDAY 9 FEBRUARY

Leaning on God

Read Psalm 28:6–9

The Lord is my strength and my shield; my heart trusts in him, and he helps me.
Psalm 28:7 (NIV)

The letter from my friend overseas was painful to read. Her husband had deserted her. They had been married for a long time and had teenage children. I reread the letter several times and decided I must answer it at once. But what could I say?

I asked God to give me the words to write back to her. So I wrote what came to mind and sent the letter. Later, I found it difficult to remember what I had written.

My friend wrote back and told me she had been standing in her kitchen crying the day my letter arrived. She would occasionally look up at the grey wintry sky that seemed to match her mood. As she washed the breakfast dishes she sensed an inner voice gently saying, 'Just lean back on me. I will support you. I am your strength.'

When my letter was delivered, she opened it and was amazed to read the words I had offered her: 'God is with you. Just lean back on him. He will support you. He is your strength.' Truly God had given me the words to comfort and encourage my grieving friend.

Prayer: *Dear Lord, we thank you for being our constant companion and strength. Help us to bring all anxiety to you so that we may find your peace. Amen*

Thought for the day: Whatever the day may bring, I am in God's loving care.

Dorothy O'Neill (South Australia, Australia)

PRAYER FOCUS: THOSE DEALING WITH BROKEN RELATIONSHIPS

FRIDAY 10 FEBRUARY

Staying Connected

Read Hebrews 10:19–25

And let us consider how we may spur one another on towards love and good deeds, not giving up meeting together, as some are in the habit of doing, but encouraging one another.
Hebrews 10:25 (NIV)

I was responsible for maintaining a large aquarium in our office reception area. Recently, because I was very busy, I became negligent in looking after the fish; the water needed cleaning and many of the fish were inactive and not alert. Immediately I scooped them up, put them in a bucket of water, and began to clean the tank and the filter mechanism. Finally I began refilling and restocking the tank before putting the fish back.

While tending to this work, I turned to God. 'I'm sorry, Lord,' I prayed, 'I've neglected this tank, and the fish have paid the price.' I realised then, in the same way, how important it is to pray and read the Bible daily so that we do not lose contact with God. Failing to join in weekly worship and fellowship isolates us from our family of faith. To be a faithful disciple of Christ requires constant care and attention to our connection to God and to others. Without these connections, we are in danger of becoming spiritually inactive and missing out on all that God has in store for us.

Prayer: *Thank you, dear Lord, for your abundant care and love. Help us to remain true and faithful, always ready to serve you. In Jesus' name we pray. Amen*

Thought for the day: Moving toward others with love is moving toward God.

Floyd Twilley (Maryland, US)

PRAYER FOCUS: THOSE WITHOUT A CHURCH FAMILY

SATURDAY 11 FEBRUARY

Sleeping in Peace

Read Psalm 4:3–8
When you are disturbed… ponder it on your beds, and be silent… I will both lie down and sleep in peace; for you alone, O Lord, make me lie down in safety.
Psalm 4:4, 8 (NRSV)

Many years ago I took my children to study in South Africa because my country was consumed by war. I found them a place to stay and found a pastor who would give them spiritual support. A few years later, when I went back to visit my children, I found that my younger daughter could not get a visa to remain in South Africa. We, along with some members of the church, prayed two days without ceasing. But we did not get the answer we needed from the immigration service.

When I came home later that night, tired and exhausted, I lay down in bed and prayed: 'Lord, help me not to be discouraged. Please show me the way to solve this situation with my daughter.' Later, in my sleep I heard a voice calling my name, but when I got up I did not see anybody. I went back to sleep and had a dream in which someone told me to read the verse quoted above. Then I understood that God wanted me to be silent and to listen.

The next day after a short interview with an immigration officer, my daughter received a visa so that she could finish her studies. This experience strengthened my belief in prayer. If we pray with faith, we can rely on God and expect an answer according to his will.

Prayer: *Gracious and merciful God, help us not to be discouraged. Help us to hear and follow your call. We pray in Jesus' name. Amen*

Thought for the day: When I trust in God, I will not be discouraged.

Madalena Manuel Simão (Luanda, Angola)

PRAYER FOCUS: FAMILIES WHO ARE SEPARATED

SUNDAY 12 FEBRUARY

Leaving the Past Behind

Read Philippians 3:13–14
Forget the former things; do not dwell on the past.
Isaiah 43:18 (NIV)

I have a habit of living in the past. I find myself wondering how my life would have turned out if I had done things differently. What if I had learned to drive earlier? What if I had gone to a different college or chosen a different subject to study? My world becomes focused on 'what ifs' instead of what is.

Sometimes these thoughts turn to the sins I have committed. I start dwelling on them and become consumed by guilt. I begin repeatedly asking God for forgiveness. I forget that he has already forgiven me and I can move forward unburdened by past sins.

God does not want any of us to live in the past. With his forgiveness, we can leave our past mistakes behind and live for today. We can enjoy the present as we experience God's love.

Prayer: *Dear God, thank you for your love and forgiveness that frees us from our past. Help us to live in the present. As Jesus taught us, we pray, 'Our Father which art in heaven, Hallowed be thy name. Thy kingdom come. Thy will be done in earth, as it is in heaven. Give us this day our daily bread. And forgive us our debts, as we forgive our debtors. And lead us not into temptation, but deliver us from evil: For thine is the kingdom, and the power, and the glory, for ever.'* Amen*

Thought for the day: With God's grace I do not have to dwell on the past.

Patrick Castleberry (Mississippi, US)

PRAYER FOCUS: THOSE STRUGGLING TO LIVE IN THE PRESENT
* Matthew 6:9–13, KJV

MONDAY 13 FEBRUARY

Faith without Fanfare

Read Matthew 6:1–4

Jesus said, 'I am with you always, even unto the end of the world.'
Matthew 28:20 (KJV)

When I was a young girl, I thought God lived at our church. After all, that was the place where most people dressed well and acted with kindness and patience, as if God had an eye on them on Sunday mornings. As I grew older, I learned that God is everywhere and actually resides within us if we invite him into our hearts. He is always with us and watches over us all the time.

I remember being amazed when I became aware that God is sincerely interested in us every day, not only when we're wearing our Sunday best. He sees into our hearts and knows our innermost thoughts every day of the week.

God smiles when we perform small acts of kindness behind the scenes, without expecting anything in return. He approves when we help an elderly neighbour to carry her groceries, when we feed a stray cat every night or when we silently pray for a stranger. I'm glad to know that God's presence is not limited to one place or to one day of the week.

Prayer: *Dear God, help us to please you through our actions today. Amen*

Thought for the day: God smiles on our quiet acts of faith.

Kay L. Campbell (Connecticut, US)

PRAYER FOCUS: CHILDREN IN CHURCH

TUESDAY 14 FEBRUARY

Body of Christ

Read 1 Corinthians 12:20–27
We are hard pressed on every side, but not crushed; perplexed but not in despair; persecuted, but not abandoned; struck down, but not destroyed.
2 Corinthians 4:8–9 (NIV)

One evening, my wife and I were sitting in a concert hall listening to beautiful music. Suddenly, my mobile phone flashed silently to tell me that someone was calling, and I saw it was my daughter. I was worried, because she never calls me at that time. When I spoke to her after the concert, the peace in my heart was broken. The news was worse than we ever could have expected.

'Dad, Andy has died suddenly of a heart attack.'

Andy, our son-in-law, was a wonderful man. He taught and mentored high school students. His life was a witness to his love for God.

The next day, we were on a plane to England to be with our daughter and three grandchildren. We experienced so much love and great help from many friends. Andy's students wrote wonderful things about him, and we pray that they will bear the fruits of the faith they learned from him. While our time was full of mourning, we experienced how great it is to be a part of the body of Christ. We felt just how powerful the love of God is when it is shown through his people.

Prayer: *Dear God, we know you are always with us. Help us to remember the power of your love in difficult times. Amen*

Thought for the day: Today I will give thanks that I am part of the body of Christ.

Zbigniew Chojnacki (Warmia-Masuria, Poland)

PRAYER FOCUS: TEACHERS

WEDNESDAY 15 FEBRUARY

Eternal Light

Read John 1:1–18

When Jesus spoke… to the people, he said, 'I am the light of the world. Whoever follows me will never walk in darkness, but will have the light of life.'

John 8:12 (NIV)

Honey bees navigate by the position of the sun. I thought of this while sitting in our tent one night, watching a trapped bee trying to get back to its hive the only way it knew how. But it was dark outside; the brightest light the bee could see was our lantern. It buzzed around the top of the tent, flying toward our hanging light again and again—sometimes crashing into it, sometimes veering away at the last second. Maybe the bee mistook the light for the sun which would have helped it find the way back to the hive.

It's easy to watch this scene and think, 'What's that bee doing?' or 'That's the wrong light!' But how often do we humans follow the wrong light and trust it to get us where we want to go? How often do we trust money, family or power and think that it will get us where we need to be, instead of trusting God as our guide? When everything seems dim, it's easy to trust in the first light we see—something that makes us feel safe or more in control again. But God is the only one who can help us out of the darkness and guide us to true freedom.

Prayer: *Dear God, help us to follow your light, the true light of Jesus Christ. In his name we pray. Amen*

Thought for the day: Today I will follow the true light that comes from God.

Alina Kanaski (Arizona, US)

PRAYER FOCUS: BEEKEEPERS

THURSDAY 16 FEBRUARY

God Is Watching

Read Matthew 6:25–34

The Lord watches over you—the Lord is your shade at your right hand.
Psalm 121:5 (NIV)

Thirteen years ago, I suffered a severe stroke. I was only 52 and in good health. A brain stem stroke left me totally paralysed from the neck down and without the ability to talk or eat. Within two minutes, my life had changed.

I spent the next year trying to regain some of what I had lost. God was watching over me. I went from a drooling, motionless person unable to breathe without an oxygen machine to someone able to breathe on her own and to move her head. After a year's hard work, I was able to go home. But what was next for me? TV or music all day? I tried that for the first few years; but I wasn't content without keeping my mind active. Again, God was watching over me and provided through a friend a way for me to function with more independence. I can now control my wheelchair with my head and headrest. And every letter and word of this story was written with the use of my eyes.

God is watching over us and sees what we need—whether another person or even a machine—to help us express our thoughts.

Prayer: *Thank you, God, for watching over us in times of need. Amen*

Thought for the day: God is watching over me today.

Gail Babula (New Jersey, US)

FRIDAY 17 FEBRUARY

God's Gifts

Read 1 Corinthians 12:7–31

To each one the manifestation of the Spirit is given for the common good.
1 Corinthians 12:7 (NIV)

My sister is a retired English as a Second Language (ESL) teacher, and I am a retired nurse. We have recently become involved in meeting the needs of refugees. Trying to meet their needs can be hard work, but we remember that we are following Jesus by serving others.

We all approach life and mission work in different ways. Some may be on the go all the time, helping at every opportunity. Others may need lots of quiet, reflective time in order to accomplish their work.

I tend to compare myself to others who serve and feel I never measure up. But this notion is not from God. Today's verse tells us that each of us has a gift we can use to help one another.

God does not expect us to have the same skills or energy levels as anyone else. When we recognise that God gave us each a gift meant just for us (see 1 Corinthians 12:11), we can put this gift to use in serving one another and the Lord.

Prayer: *Dear God, thank you for giving us gifts and talents. Help us to use them to honour you. Amen*

Thought for the day: How am I using my gifts to serve God?

Nancy R. Meyer (Nebraska, US)

PRAYER FOCUS: REFUGEES

SATURDAY 18 FEBRUARY

Blessed Assurance

Read Philippians 1:18–30

For to me, to live is Christ, and to die is gain.
Philippians 1:21 (NIV)

My friend Glenn had been diagnosed with leukaemia and was in hospital for chemotherapy. As I drove to visit him, I thought about what the visit might be like. I have visited other friends who have been sent to hospital unexpectedly, and sometimes it is difficult. People reacting to the diagnosis of a potentially fatal disease may show anger, depression or grief. While Glenn had always been a very positive person, I didn't expect him to be in the best of moods when I entered his hospital ward.

I shouldn't have been concerned. That first visit was an uplifting experience, as were my other visits over the next several weeks. Most of the time Glenn was upbeat, welcoming visitors and joking with the hospital staff. Although his future was uncertain, he was at peace. As he told me, 'If my time is up, it's OK. I know where I am going.' Glenn's response was a great example of what faith can do.

Although the apostle Paul was imprisoned in chains and uncertain whether he would live or die, he saw the blessings of either outcome. He was at peace because he trusted in God. We will all face challenges, but if we have accepted Christ as our Saviour, we do not face those challenges alone. In whatever circumstance, we can find peace and assurance from knowing that our Lord and Saviour is with us today and throughout eternity.

Prayer: *Heavenly Father, we thank you for your presence in our lives, for the comfort and peace you provide in times of trouble. Help us to share the good news of your love and grace with others. Amen*

Thought for the day: God says, 'Never will I leave you; never will I forsake you' (see Hebrews 13:5).

John Bown (Minnesota, US)

PRAYER FOCUS: THOSE UNDERGOING CHEMOTHERAPY

SUNDAY 19 FEBRUARY

Never Off Duty

Read Luke 10:30–37

We are God's handiwork, created in Christ Jesus to do good works, which God prepared in advance for us to do.
Ephesians 2:10 (NIV)

Recently I met my son for lunch. To my surprise, he insisted on paying for my meal, saying, 'Give the money to someone who really needs it.' After lunch we parted, and I started for the railway station. Suddenly, I heard a quiet voice behind me saying, 'Excuse me.' I turned to see a young man. He needed a hostel bed for the night and asked for some money. As I listened to his story, I felt sure that God wanted me to help him. I gave him the money that I had expected to spend on lunch, shook his hand and promised to pray for him. He thanked me warmly.

Later, as I travelled on the train, I knew that Jesus had been present in the cafe with my son and me. I knew Jesus was also there on the street, meeting me in that young man.

Sometimes after doing a good deed, I feel as if I can go 'off duty'. But in a way, I am separating my life into compartments—this much for God, the rest for myself. This experience reminded me that God never goes 'off duty'. He calls us to share love and compassion at any time, in any place.

Prayer: *Thank you, Lord, that you are always available to help us. May we be ready to respond to your prompting to help others, whenever and wherever that may be. In Jesus' name. Amen*

Thought for the day: God has prepared a way for me to serve others today.

Hazel Fitz-Gibbon (Surrey, England)

PRAYER FOCUS: THOSE WHO ARE HOMELESS

MONDAY 20 FEBRUARY

Waiting for the Lord

Read Psalm 27:1–14

Wait for the Lord; be strong, and let your heart take courage; wait for the Lord!
Psalm 27:14 (NRSV)

David, the presumed author of Psalm 27, had adversaries who were intent on taking his life; yet he proclaimed that the Lord was his light, his salvation and his stronghold. I do not have enemies threatening my life, but I have been afraid of a raging storm, an uncomfortable task or a frightening medical diagnosis.

I would like to say that the first thoughts that come to mind when I am faced with a challenge are 'Be strong… Wait for the Lord', but my reaction is usually a tightening in my stomach and worry that circles through my mind. I'm afraid. In those times it helps me to personalise this psalm by changing the word 'whom' to 'what' in verse 1: 'what shall I fear?'; 'of what shall I be afraid?' Then I remember that I am not alone. I can 'wait for the Lord'. Even though I am weak, 'the Lord is the stronghold of my life' (Psalm 27:1). I do not feel strong in myself, but I know that the Lord is with me.

As I look back over my life, I have experienced the strength and love of God through the hands, words and prayers of other people, the strength and love of others in my life. God understands what we are going through. Even when we are unable to utter anything more than the phrase 'The Lord is my strength', we can remember that we are connected to a loving God.

Prayer: *Dear Lord, we give thanks that you are the stronghold of our lives and that we need not be afraid. Amen*

Thought for the day: Today I will remember that the Lord is my strength.

Dot French (New Jersey, US)

TUESDAY 21 FEBRUARY

The Father's Business

Read Luke 2:41–52
Jesus said to his parents, '[Know] ye not that I must be about my Father's business?'
Luke 2:49 (KJV)

While reading about the prophet Anna in Luke's Gospel, I felt guilty. A widow, Anna 'did not depart from the temple, but served God with fastings and prayers night and day' (Luke 2:37). I'm also a widow but have never spent a whole day praying, let alone fasting. Was I failing God? As I continued to read, I came across the story of twelve-year-old Jesus disappearing during a family trip to Jerusalem. Three days later, when his parents found him in the temple and demanded an explanation, Jesus simply replied, '[Know] ye not that I must be about my Father's business?'

'That's right!' I thought. Even though I didn't pray all day and night like Anna, I could still be about my Father's business. It means responding to the guidance of the Holy Spirit. That's something I can do, if I'll just follow Jesus' example. Jesus persistently sought the Father's will. At first I thought that might be difficult. Yet, as I spend time in prayer, meditation and studying scripture, I'm grasping the way God communicates with me. Then, as I act in faith, I'm trusting the Holy Spirit to guide me in my Father's business.

God has given each of us important tasks. Each day we can ask God for guidance and follow where that leads, believing that 'the one who began a good work among you will bring it to completion' (Philippians 1:6).

Prayer: *Thank you, Father, for guiding our steps so that our lives reflect your glory. Amen*

Thought for the day: How am I going about the Father's business?

Laura L. Bradford (Washington, US)

PRAYER FOCUS: WIDOWS

WEDNESDAY 22 FEBRUARY

The Prayers of Many People

Read James 5:13–16
The prayer of a righteous person is powerful and effective.
James 5:16 (NIV)

Recently my wife, Joyce, went through a difficult time with serious health issues. We made a trip to the hospital in Minnesota to deal with one specific health concern. However, while the medical staff were preparing to respond, they discovered other serious medical problems. The result was that our stay lasted for 25 days, and the real purpose for our going to the area in the first place could not be addressed at that time.

Generally, I do not like waiting for issues to be addressed. However, during our stay, I felt a peace that all things were working for our good (see Romans 8:28). I have often wondered whether the number of people praying for a particular concern makes a difference in God's response to that need. Certainly God hears and responds to the prayer of a single person. But will he be more apt to satisfy that need if hundreds of people are praying? I cannot say that I would have felt more fearful had only one person been praying for us. But I know that my peace came from knowing of the large number of people who were holding us up to God through their prayers.

Prayer: *All-knowing God, we thank you for hearing the prayers of your people. Help us to realise that there is much power in prayer. Amen*

Thought for the day: Today I will add my prayers to those of others.

Stanley L. Hayes (Michigan, US)

PRAYER FOCUS: THOSE EXPERIENCING SERIOUS HEALTH ISSUES

THURSDAY 23 FEBRUARY

Love Your Neighbour

Read Mark 12:28–31

Jesus said, 'I was naked and you gave me clothing, I was sick and you took care of me, I was in prison and you visited me.'
Matthew 25:36 (NRSV)

I have been a regular reader of The Upper Room for over eight years. I feel comforted and strengthened in my faith by reserving 30 minutes of my day to pray, read and reflect on the word of God, our guide and protector.

Through my devotional reading, I have come to believe that God calls all of us to help our neighbours. By helping others we follow Christ's example and reflect his love to the world. One day I decided follow this call by visiting a young man who had been in prison for more than a year. When I arrived, I saw people who were in need of spiritual and material care.

This experience reminded me that committing to social action is something everyone can do. As Christians we can offer help not only by giving material goods but also through prayers, spiritual encouragement and acts of grace. After all, offering compassion to those in need is a gift to Christ as well.

Prayer: *O God, help us to show your love and care to those who are in difficult or desperate situations. As Jesus taught us, we pray, 'Our Father which art in heaven, Hallowed be thy name. Thy kingdom come. Thy will be done, as in heaven, so in earth. Give us day by day our daily bread. And forgive us our sins; for we also forgive every one that is indebted to us. And lead us not into temptation; but deliver us from evil.'* Amen*

Thought for the day: What can I do today to help a neighbour?

Anabela Couto de Castro Valente (Luanda, Angola)

PRAYER FOCUS: PRISONERS
* Luke 11:2–4, KJV

FRIDAY 24 FEBRUARY

Walk the Talk

Read Hebrews 11:3–12

You see that a person is shown to be righteous through faithful actions and not through faith alone.
James 2:24 (CEB)

Hebrews 11 is often referred to as 'Faith's Hall of Fame' because it lists people who fulfilled what God asked them to do. One example is Abraham who obeyed God's call to leave his home, even though he did not know anything about where he was going. Other examples are Enoch, who 'walked faithfully with God' (Genesis 5:22, 24, NIV) and Abel who offered a better sacrifice than Cain did. These and others mentioned had one thing in common: they obeyed the Lord.

James 2:20 says, 'Faith without works is dead.' The people in Hebrews 11 ultimately pleased God when they fulfilled their faith by obediently taking action. They were not perfect; they had weaknesses and temptations similar to ours. But in each case, they helped accomplish God's purposes by obedience to his call—no matter where that call led.

Our faith calls each of us to action, and in the Bible we find everything we need to help us faithfully to carry out God's will.

Prayer: *Dear God, help us put our faith into action. In Jesus' name we pray. Amen*

Thought for the day: Beyond my words, God wants my actions.

Donald Bottenfield (Pennsylvania, US)

PRAYER FOCUS: TO DISCERN GOD'S CALL

SATURDAY 25 FEBRUARY

Still Here?

Read Ecclesiastes 3:9–15

Help me understand what your precepts are about so I can contemplate your wondrous works!
Psalm 119:27 (CEB)

As a child, I would pore over maps, all the time fantasising about packing a suitcase and exploring the world. At high school, my plan of action was simple: to become a travel writer. I would taste exotic cuisine, collect unique trinkets, gain profound insights, and of course do my Christian duty by evangelising captive audiences on long flights.

Had God himself told me that years later I'd still be in Indiana, ministering to teenagers no less, I probably would not have believed it. But here I am, and I'm discovering that the wonders of the world that I had once sought are displayed in the gradually shifting culture just beyond my front door.

I'm not where I intended to be or doing the things I once dreamed I'd do. Sometimes I wrestle with resentment about the direction life has taken. But I can say with confidence that God's extraordinary presence is not banned from ordinary places. Discovering admirable, excellent and praiseworthy things (see Philippians 4:8) doesn't require travelling far. It just requires following God's purpose for our gifts and abilities wherever he may lead. I might not be where I expected to be, but God is doing great things where I am and letting me be a part of it. That's an adventure I'm excited to stay here for.

Prayer: *Dear God, help us see the beautiful things you are doing around us wherever we are. Amen*

Thought for the day: How has God changed and exceeded my plans?

Megan L. Anderson (Indiana, US)

PRAYER FOCUS: THOSE WHO FEEL DISCONTENTED

SUNDAY 26 FEBRUARY

Renewed Day by Day

Read 2 Corinthians 4:8–18

If anyone is in Christ, the new creation has come: The old has gone, the new is here!
2 Corinthians 5:17 (NIV)

I struggle with an illness that saps my strength and energy. As a result, I have had difficulty getting myself out of bed in the morning. A friend sent me a picture of a phoenix with the words, 'Still I rise.' I added today's verse and 2 Corinthians 4:16: 'Therefore we do not lose heart. Though outwardly we are wasting away, yet inwardly we are being renewed day by day.' I use it as a bookmark and keep it by my bed.

Many of us go through trying times, whether dealing with illness, limitations or the emotions of accepting these realities. The words and picture on my bookmark remind me that each day is an opportunity to rise again, physically and emotionally, and to become a new creation in Christ.

Now, each morning after looking at my bookmark, I stretch my arms upward. I pray for God to fill me with the strength of the Holy Spirit as I rise and am renewed. Our transformation in Christ is an ongoing process, and each day moves us further along this path.

Prayer: *Dear Lord, help us reach to you for strength and welcome each day as an opportunity to be renewed in Jesus Christ. Amen*

Thought for the day: Each day is an opportunity to be renewed in Christ.

Scott Martin (New Jersey, US)

PRAYER FOCUS: THOSE SUFFERING FROM CHRONIC FATIGUE

MONDAY 27 FEBRUARY

Dancing Lament

Read Psalm 61:1–4

Hear my voice, O God, in my complaint; preserve my life from the dread enemy.
Psalm 64:1 (NRSV)

I teach a dance class each week in which we move our bodies in different ways to express emotions, including negative ones. We bring our hands high above our heads and then move them quickly to the ground as if we're throwing down a large, heavy object to let go of our pain, anger, irritation or complacency in an active and physical way.

Teaching this form of dance has taught me how important it is for us to have a way to release our negative thoughts and feelings without guilt, shame or remorse. After a recent class session, one of my students said, 'Now that I've danced and released, everything is much clearer.' Practices such as this allow us to connect with our feelings, whether we need to cry out and complain to God or to give him our thanks and praise.

The authors of lamentation psalms like today's reading cry, plead and complain. The psalmists are unafraid to complain because they know God understands the need to release painful feelings. Their honest praying, like our honest dancing, is an authentic expression of our feelings and heartfelt prayers for what we need. We can trust that God receives our complaints so that we may release them and be free.

Prayer: *Loving God, thank you for the many ways we can express our thoughts and needs. Amen*

Thought for the day: God listens to both my complaints and my praise.

Claire K. McKeever-Burgett (Tennessee, US)

PRAYER FOCUS: TO PRAY HONESTLY

TUESDAY 28 FEBRUARY

Shine Like Stars

Read Philippians 2:12–16
You will shine among them like stars in the sky as you hold firmly to the word of life.
Philippians 2:15–16 (NIV)

My church has offered our members a course that encourages us and equips us to share our faith with our friends and neighbours. I usually avoid situations where I need to voice my faith to others, so this is quite a challenge for me. As I was considering the course and my feelings about evangelism, my dear friend Brenda came to mind.

Brenda was big in spirit and faith. She loved Jesus so much she shone. I was with her when she was diagnosed with cancer and was amazed when she told the specialist that she wasn't afraid to die because she loved Jesus. Wherever she was, especially in the nursing home where she spent the last few weeks of her life, Brenda was ready and happy to share her faith and love of Christ with anyone willing to listen.

I've come to realise that I've made things far too complicated. Evangelism is not about having the right words at the right time. Sharing my faith is a matter of drawing alongside others, showing them what Jesus has done in my life, and letting them know that he would like to do the same for them.

Prayer: *Heavenly Father, help us to accompany others and share with them the love and new life that Jesus offers. Amen*

Thought for the day: I can share my faith by being present with others.

Mandy Slade (Somerset, England)

PRAYER FOCUS: SOMEONE RECENTLY DIAGNOSED WITH CANCER

Prayer Workshop

Saying Yes to Possibility

Throughout his ministry, chief priests and Pharisees—and even his own disciples—confronted Jesus with the question, 'Is it lawful?' By this they meant, 'Is it right? Ethical? Approved by God? Sanctioned by society?' Sometimes people asked this question to put Jesus in the wrong. But I think that in asking this question, Jesus' opponents and followers alike were choosing the easy way out. By asking this simple, yes-or-no question, they avoided the complexity and possibilities that come with change.

In Mark 3:1–5, Jesus entered the synagogue and encountered a man with a withered hand. The Pharisees were watching, wanting to accuse Jesus. This time Jesus asked them the question: 'Is it lawful to do good or to do harm on the sabbath, to save life or to kill?' (Mark 3:4, NRSV). The Pharisees did not answer. Matthew, Mark and Luke all recounted this story, but only Mark mentioned how Jesus felt about the silence of his opponents. Verse 5 says that Jesus 'looked around at them with anger; he was grieved at their hardness of heart'.

Anger I can understand. The Pharisees were trying to trap Jesus. They showed no compassion for the man with the withered hand, and they did not even answer Jesus' question. Mark also says Jesus was grieved. The grief intrigues me. After all, Jesus still healed the man's hand. He still demonstrated that it is possible and even good to save a life and show compassion on the sabbath. He did not need the permission or approval of the Pharisees to act powerfully and heal this man.

This is a story about change. Jesus' ministry proposes a new way of interpreting the law, a new way of relating to others that is grounded in compassion. The Pharisees feared change and the unknown, and they remained silent rather than consider the possibilities raised by Jesus' question. I think that this fear was the cause of Jesus' grief. Perhaps Jesus, the son of God—who understands the fullness of God's mercy and the infinite possibility for new life with him—was grieving for opportunities and possibilities that were lost because of the Pharisees' silence. Perhaps Jesus was grieving for what might have been. If the Pharisees had said, 'Yes! Heal this man, and save a life', would Jesus have then healed not just the withered hand of this one man, but every hurt and pain and sorrow present in the synagogue? What miracle did they miss because they did not say yes to compassion and yes to possibility?

As followers of Jesus, we claim the assurance that 'in Christ, there is a new creation: everything old has passed away; see, everything has become new!' (2 Corinthians 5:17). As we move into a new year and face changes that seem to come ever more quickly, what will our response to new opportunities be? Will we release our fears and preconceived certainties and say yes to God's possibilities? This year, I want to say yes to compassion and yes to all the possibilities God offers. Will you join me?

Several meditations in this issue deal with themes of change and transformation. Consider reading the following meditations again as you reflect: January 1, 6, 9, 23, 26; February 4, 8, 25, 26; March 6, 8 and April 16.

Lindsay Gray
Editorial Director, Magazines

WEDNESDAY 1 MARCH

Ash Wednesday

Read 1 Corinthians 9:24–27
Do you not know that in a race the runners all compete, but only one receives the prize? Run in such a way that you may win it.
1 Corinthians 9:24 (NRSV)

As a former college football player, my ears perk up when Paul refers to sports. To the Corinthians Paul writes, 'Athletes exercise self-control in all things; they do it to receive a perishable wreath, but we an imperishable one' (1 Corinthians 9:25). Paul speaks of a runner and a boxer—both have to be extraordinarily disciplined in their training if they expect to win.

Every four years, over 200 countries worldwide send their very best athletes to compete in the Olympics. I love reading about the athletes and their unusual journeys of perseverance, courage and dedication. Each athlete has worked hard and has overcome obstacles to reach an elite level of competition. Their stories remind me that it is easy to be a fan but hard to be an athlete. Being a fan requires little, but being an athlete requires training and discipline.

Paul makes the same point about our life of faith. Following Jesus requires discipline and perseverance. As we enter into the season of Lent, Paul's letters remind us to practise the self-discipline necessary to grow in Jesus' likeness each day. By taking on new habits or disciplines during Lent, we can grow closer to Christ.

Prayer: *Holy God, help us to not only proclaim the name of Jesus, but to follow him with dedication and passion. Amen*

Thought for the day: What new practice can help me to grow closer to Christ?

Matt Miofsky (Missouri, US)

PRAYER FOCUS: OLYMPIC ATHLETES

THURSDAY 2 MARCH

A Precious Gift

Read Hebrews 13:7–16

I will offer to thee the sacrifice of thanksgiving, and will call upon the name of the Lord.
Psalm 116:17 (KJV)

I've always observed Lent by sacrificing something to help me remember Christ's holy sacrifice for me. But over the years some of my passion for this practice dimmed, and I began to question my motives for observing this spiritual discipline. Does Christ really find pleasure in my 'suffering'? I had to acknowledge the answer was a resounding no. After all, Christ loves me!

Divided between the desire to make a heartfelt offering to God and the ambivalence I felt, I struggled. I yearned to give God what I considered most precious—and with some reluctance, I realised that most precious to me is my time. Most days I feel I don't have a second to spare.

Committing to give God an hour daily is a genuine sacrifice—but like everything I've given in the past, my time already belongs to God. Those 60 minutes—bowing in prayer, reading the Bible or volunteering—leave me stronger and happier. I now share a more intimate relationship with Christ than I've enjoyed in years. I haven't really given up anything after all. I've discovered the riches of time well spent in the presence of God.

Prayer: *Dear Lord, thank you for your sacrifice and for the blessing we find when we move closer to you, day by day, hour by hour. Amen*

Thought for the day: One of the greatest gifts I can give to God is my time.

Heidi Gaul (Oregon, US)

PRAYER FOCUS: VOLUNTEERS

FRIDAY 3 MARCH

Sombre Optimism

Read Joel 2:12–17

Job answered the Lord, 'I had heard of you by the hearing of the ear, but now my eye sees you; therefore I despise myself, and repent in dust and ashes.'
Job 42:5–6 (NRSV)

During the Ash Wednesday service at my church, my minister alternates between two different statements when imposing the cross of ashes on the forehead of worshippers. The first is, 'Remember that you are dust, and to dust you shall return.' The second is, 'Repent, and believe the gospel.' In my church's tradition, the thanksgiving over the ashes includes this petition: 'Grant that these ashes may be to us a sign of our mortality and penitence.'

Sin and death are not exactly popular topics and many people believe that Ash Wednesday is unnecessarily sombre and pessimistic. However, I see it as a healthy response to the realities of life. During the service we are invited to contemplate our sin and our death and to confess our sinfulness because we are confident in God's grace and forgiveness. We contemplate our death because of our confidence in Christ's victory over the grave.

Ash Wednesday is sombre but optimistic. It allows us to face life as it really is with God's promise of our deliverance from sin and death.

Prayer: *Almighty God, help us to remember that only by your gracious gift are we given everlasting life. We pray through Jesus Christ our Saviour. Amen*

Thought for the day: Ash Wednesday is an invitation to remember God's grace.

Michael A. Macdonald (North Carolina, US)

PRAYER FOCUS: THOSE WHO HAVE NOT FOUND HOPE IN JESUS

SATURDAY 4 MARCH

Missed Opportunity

Read Colossians 4:2–6

Be wise in the way you act toward outsiders; make the most of every opportunity.
Colossians 4:5 (NIV)

I've become accustomed to television coverage of sporting events using instant replay. But real life has no instant replay. If we miss the moment, it's gone. I realised this a few years ago while watching our grandson play cricket. My late husband and I didn't love cricket, but we loved our grandson so we went to his match.

I took along some books to pass some time; the game started at 9.00 am and was due to finish around 4.30 pm. I made the mistake of thinking not much was happening, because Brendan wasn't bowling or batting. But I heard the cheer and discovered I was wrong. Brendan had made a spectacular catch and I'd missed it. There was no replay. I would never have the opportunity to see that particular catch.

How often do we miss opportunities? We sometimes forget to pray for someone, to phone a friend at a crucial time, to visit someone who needs our help or to smile at a stranger. We often miss the chance to share our faith. The Holy Spirit prompts us, but if we're not paying attention and obeying, that opportunity may be missed for ever. When we pay attention, we are given many opportunities to share our faith and serve and support one another.

Prayer: *Dear heavenly Father, help us to listen for your Holy Spirit's promptings, ready to obey so that we may take every opportunity to serve you. Amen*

Thought for the day: When we pay attention, we see many opportunities to serve God.

Lenore Warton (New South Wales, Australia)

PRAYER FOCUS: GRANDPARENTS AND GRANDCHILDREN

SUNDAY 5 MARCH

First Sunday in Lent

Read Romans 10:8–13
If you declare with your mouth, 'Jesus is Lord,' and believe in your heart that God raised him from the dead, you will be saved.
Romans 10:9 (NIV)

Choosing God was the best decision I ever made. Looking back, I can remember a time when I felt alone and insecure about my future. I had more questions than answers and thought I had no one to help me fill the void in my life.

One day I had a life-changing experience: I accepted Jesus into my heart. I soon began to see a change within me and a change around me. The more I sought the Lord, the more I learned about myself: my gifts, how unique I am and how much God loves me. My world went from being a blur to a much clearer picture.

Now, I tell my story so that I may invite others to seek the Lord with all of their hearts. I challenge those around me to share their stories with others. When we allow God to direct us in everything we do, we encourage others to do the same.

Prayer: *Dear Jesus, thank you for guiding us on our journeys of faith. Help us to show others the way to you. We pray as you taught us, saying, 'Our Father which art in heaven, Hallowed be thy name. Thy kingdom come. Thy will be done in earth, as it is in heaven. Give us this day our daily bread. And forgive us our debts, as we forgive our debtors. And lead us not into temptation, but deliver us from evil: For thine is the kingdom, and the power, and the glory, for ever.'* Amen'*

Thought for the day: Today I will share my faith with someone else.

Sally Perez (Washington, US)

PRAYER FOCUS: NEW BELIEVERS
* Matthew 6:9–13, KJV

MONDAY 6 MARCH

A Simple Act of Faith

Read Matthew 14:22–32

When [Peter] saw the wind, he was afraid and, beginning to sink, cried out, 'Lord, save me!' Immediately Jesus reached out his hand and caught him. 'You of little faith,' he said, 'why did you doubt?'
Matthew 14:30–31 (NIV)

When things are going well, it is easier to be happy and to believe in God's goodness and care. The real test comes when our good fortune or happiness suddenly changes—when, like a stormy sea, life seems to turn against us.

We all go through these experiences: disappointment and disillusionment, loss or betrayal, the agony of illness, the vulnerability of old age. Any of these can plunge us into a state of anxiety and despair. Like Peter in our reading for today, we can become overwhelmed and sink into doubt about God's protective care.

But we can also learn from Peter's actions by calling to Jesus. Then, even if we falter as Peter did, we can reach out to the one who walked on the sea and calmed the waters (Matthew 8:26). No matter how threatening or confusing our circumstances may become, the good and loving Shepherd knows us and has promised to lead and protect us even when we go through the valley of the shadow of death (see Psalm 23:4).

Remembering these examples, we are encouraged to act in faith and turn to God in prayer. Believers through the ages have testified that God will help us to deal with our challenges in new and hopeful ways.

Prayer: *Dear God, help us to look beyond our own capabilities and to trust you to show us a more excellent way. Amen*

Thought for the day: With Christ I can face any problem imaginable.

Carel Anthonissen (Cape Town, South Africa)

PRAYER FOCUS: THOSE WHO MAKE THEIR LIVING ON THE SEA

TUESDAY 7 MARCH

We Are Family

Read Romans 8:14–17
God destined us to be his adopted children through Jesus Christ because of his love. This was according to his goodwill and plan.
Ephesians 1:5 (CEB)

I was born the daughter of an unwed teenager who decided to give me up for adoption. A couple who had always wanted children, but couldn't have any, decided they wanted to adopt. God answered their prayers when they were granted permission to adopt me. God was watching over me too; I couldn't have asked for better parents. They brought me up in a loving Christian home. They always set a good example for me and taught me right from wrong.

My mother was with me for only 13 years when she died unexpectedly. With God's help, my dad did a great job of raising me. He lived for many more years and was able to walk me down the aisle and have a close relationship with my children.

My parents loved me unconditionally. My birth mother's decision to allow me to be adopted was also a selfless act of love. She put me first, and I will always be grateful for this glimpse of God's love. God offers us unconditional love, support, and forgiveness; he fulfils our needs and never fails us. When we profess our faith in Christ, we become part of God's family.

Prayer: *Heavenly Father, watch over all parents and children. Thank you for adopting us into your family. Amen*

Thought for the day: Who has shown me God's unconditional love?

Mary Ann Baker (Pennsylvania, US)

PRAYER FOCUS: FAMILIES IN THE PROCESS OF ADOPTION

WEDNESDAY 8 MARCH

How Does Your Garden Grow?

Read Isaiah 55:10–13

If anyone is in Christ, the new creation has come: The old has gone, the new is here!
2 Corinthians 5:17 (NIV)

Where I live, March is a month of changes. Spring wants to pop through, but winter isn't quite finished with us. I get restless during the month of March: my hands itch to dig in the dirt. I see tiny shoots of green in my garden. Birds are chirping again and the sun seems a little brighter each day.

So I begin preparing for spring and summer planting. I clean pots, sharpen my tools, prepare the soil and earmark seed catalogues that have new ideas for my gardens.

But then I remember my spiritual garden. Am I sharpening the tools of meditation, scripture reading and prayer? Am I making an inventory of the new ways I can share God with the world around me? Am I preparing the soil in my life for new and exciting challenges for personal growth?

During the month of March and the season of Lent, I see the promise of new life in my garden, and I remember the promise of new life in Christ. By preparing for God's new creation during the season of Lent, we can experience new life sprouting within us: life that can bring us new joy and give hope to those around us.

Prayer: *Dear God of all being, may we tend the soil of our souls so that we can receive the new life you are cultivating in each of us. In Jesus' name. Amen*

Thought for the day: God continues to cultivate new life in me each day.

Lauri Ricker (Maryland, US)

PRAYER FOCUS: GARDENERS

THURSDAY 9 MARCH

Serving at Any Age

Read 1 Peter 4:8–11

Each of you should use whatever gift you have received to serve others, as faithful stewards of God's grace in its various forms.
1 Peter 4:10 (NIV)

Following a series of major surgeries, my older brother reminded me that growing old 'isn't for wimps'. Many of us will eventually have to deal with the struggles of ageing. But there can be a silver lining. Generally, in our later years, we retire or work less and have more time to devote to our spiritual life. So ageing isn't necessarily something to fear, because it is a time when we can flourish in serving the Lord.

My brother, who is 82 years old, is a good example of serving others as his body will allow. He works with various charities at his church and in his neighbourhood and recently took a seriously ill friend to the hospital and waited while he underwent surgery. Everyone can serve no matter what their circumstances. Even if we have to use a stick or a walker, we can visit an ailing friend or make hospital visits, and we can always pray for others. When we share the love of Christ by caring for those who are ill or disabled and by encouraging their carers, God blesses all of us.

If we make it a point to be aware of the many needs around us, we can find many ways to serve our Lord. God has equipped each of us in some way to be an agent of grace.

Prayer: *Dear Lord, help us to love and care for others as you care for us. Amen*

Thought for the day: Regardless of my age, I can serve the Lord.

Walter N. Maris (Missouri, US)

PRAYER FOCUS: PEOPLE ABOUT TO RETIRE

FRIDAY 10 MARCH

God's Feast

Read 1 Corinthians 11:23–34
Everyone ate until they were full. They filled twelve baskets with the leftover pieces of bread and fish.
Mark 6:42–43 (CEB)

Together, my family and I attended an evening church service. We participated in the service with reverence and wholeheartedly dedicated our praise to God. We offered prayers and listened to our minister preach the good news.

Then it was time for the sacrament of Holy Communion. The congregation was large, so we ran out of Communion bread. A woman sitting next to me decided to split her piece of Communion bread and give me half. I accepted it gratefully. Together we enjoyed a banquet of love, which brings us into communion with Christ. Through this woman's action, I witnessed an example of God's love. Even during times of shortage or scarcity, God's love does not run out.

Prayer: *Dear ever-loving God, guide us to express your love even when circumstances seem to work against us. Amen*

Thought for the day: My Christian community can show me God's abundant love.

Maria Natalie (Jakarta, Indonesia)

PRAYER FOCUS: CHRISTIANS IN INDONESIA

SATURDAY 11 MARCH

Strength for the Battle

Read Isaiah 40:27–31

You created my inmost being; you knit me together in my mother's womb.
Psalm 139:13 (NIV)

When she was two weeks old, my daughter had open-heart surgery to repair a rare congenital defect. For the next two months, she fought for her life. Every day was a struggle. During that time, I learned to rely on God for both my strength and my daughter's health.

Life is precious and fragile, and sometimes too short; but our will to live is strong. God has created our intricate bodies to be strong and resilient.

Over the next year, my daughter continued her battle for life. A common cold put her back in the hospital for weeks. Once again I called out to God to give both of us strength, and he faithfully provided it.

Our Creator knows the struggles we face. God has known us from the moment our lives began and knows us better than anyone. We can fight through life's challenges on our own, or we can battle them with God. He longs for us to call for the strength we need to fight our battles. He who knows our inmost being waits ready to give us the strength we need.

Prayer: *Dear God, you created us and know every part of us. Alone, we are not strong; but with you we can endure the challenges of life. Amen*

Thought for the day: Today I will ask God to be my strength.

Sarah Lyons (Kansas, US)

PRAYER FOCUS: PAEDIATRIC SURGEONS

SUNDAY 12 MARCH

Second Sunday in Lent

Read Matthew 4:1-11
My thoughts are not your thoughts, nor are your ways my ways, says the Lord.
Isaiah 55:8 (NRSV)

I tend to be a slow learner, and I also tend to think that I know what's best. As a teenager, I sometimes did what I wanted to do instead of listening to my parents. Now as an adult, I sometimes do what I want to do instead of listening to God. Even after being left broken, hurt or empty countless times as a result of listening only to myself, I still struggle to obey God.

In today's reading, the tempter tries three times to convince Jesus to give in to temptation instead of listening to God. Each of the three times, instead of listening to these words, Jesus speaks God's truth. Even though the offers are enticing, Jesus knows that God's ways are better.

Today, we may be tempted to cut corners at work or to lower our standards in relationships or to shirk our commitments instead of being faithful. We are often tempted to do what we think is easier instead of listening to God.

Even though I am still a slow learner, I have come to realise that no matter how much sense my ways make, they always lead to brokenness. When we follow God's ways things may not be easier, but the result is always better. God's ways lead to wholeness and life every time.

Prayer: *Dear Lord, help us to remember your ways and follow them. Amen*

Thought for the day: Today I will rely on God instead of myself.

Adam Weber (South Dakota, US)

PRAYER FOCUS: SOMEONE STRUGGLING TO FOLLOW GOD

MONDAY 13 MARCH

To the Street

Read James 2:14–26

Whoever looks intently into the perfect law that gives freedom, and continues in it—not forgetting what they have heard, but doing it—they will be blessed in what they do.
James 1:25 (NIV)

Worshipping with fellow Christians is special. Being fed from the word of God, being taught and encouraged by singing and praying together, giving to meet the needs of others and remembering the sacrifice of our Saviour all make our time together such a blessing.

But I think that too often the motivation to live more faithfully grows cold once the church services are over. We don't always take what we learn in church and live it out in our daily lives. If we leave behind what we have learned while we were together, we miss out on putting our discipleship into practice. Taking to the street what we have learned means treating our families and neighbours the way Christ would. It means being the very best employees we can be. It means maturing as parents, as students and even as citizens. As the verse from James quoted above tells us, it means that we go beyond listening to acting.

Meeting together as Christians gives us the tools and an understanding of God's love that help us live faithfully. Wherever we go as we leave the church service, we can resolve to share with others the unity and peace that Christ's love inspires in us.

Prayer: *Dear God, help us not to take the blessings of life in Christ for granted but instead to share them with those around us. In Jesus' name. Amen*

Thought for the day: Along with worship and fellowship, God wants our discipleship and service.

Andy Baker (Tennessee, US)

PRAYER FOCUS: THOSE WITHOUT A CHURCH HOME

TUESDAY 14 MARCH

All God's Children

Read Revelation 7:9–17
Peter began to speak: 'I now realise how true it is that God does not show favouritism but accepts from every nation the one who fears him and does what is right.'
Acts 10:34–35 (NIV)

The coffin was carried in, and the family followed in a seemingly never-ending stream. All the seats in the big church were filled. Margaret had always loved children, and in some sense she would have considered each person there her child. She mothered her biological children and was the beloved foster mother of many. With her husband, Vic, she gave these children a loving Christian home. Not content with that, the two also arranged summer holidays for children who could not afford them.

Vic and Margaret's foster children were of many different ethnicities and backgrounds. Over the years, they had experienced problems and arguments like any family, but that day they all came to honour the beloved mother who had given them such a good start in life and taught them to love God and one another.

Surely it will be like that when we meet around God's throne, but at that time the mourning will be gone. And what a diverse crowd we will be—all children of the same Father but from every tribe and nation—coming to love and worship our loving God!

Prayer: *Thank you, Lord, for offering your love and salvation to each of us, your children, without preference or judgement. Amen*

Thought for the day: How can I embrace my heavenly family here on earth?

Marion Turnbull (Liverpool, England)

WEDNESDAY 15 MARCH

Welcoming the Stranger

Read Leviticus 19:32–34
Let mutual love continue. Do not neglect to show hospitality to strangers, for by doing that some have entertained angels without knowing it.
Hebrews 13:1–2 (NRSV)

I once led a group that met twice a week for lunch at the local community college. One day a new student sat down at the far end of our table. As a minister trying to build relationships with the students, I saw this as a wonderful opportunity. 'Is this your first term here?' I inquired. 'Yes,' she replied softly. As we continued the conversation we learned that she was from China and had been in the USA for only four months. 'We meet here every Tuesday and Thursday. If you would like to eat with us, you are more than welcome,' I told her. As she got up to leave I said, 'I hope to see you next Tuesday!' uncertain if I would see her again.

The next Tuesday came and so did she. I was happy to see that she had brought a friend—a student from India, also new to the country. Providing community, support and a place for the new students to practise English was a gift God gave us to share with them. And their gift to us was their openness to share their culture and to give us the chance to entertain angels.

Prayer: *Dear God, help us to overcome social barriers so that we can participate in your work in the world. Amen*

Thought for the day: I can share God's love by inviting others into my life.

Kathryn Helms (Maryland, US)

PRAYER FOCUS: INTERNATIONAL STUDENTS

THURSDAY 16 MARCH

Planting God's Love

Read Psalm 90:12–17

May the favour of the Lord our God rest on us; establish the work of our hands for us.
Psalm 90:17 (NIV)

As a young man I suffered a series of losses and failures that left me with a hard heart. The God I had known as a youth seemed to have disappeared. Thankfully, when I began to date the woman who became my wife, my life began to change. She saw something good in me and planted the seed of God's love in my life. With time and nurturing, the seed grew into an understanding that even though I had turned my back on God, he hadn't left me.

It took several years of Christian love and my wife's leading, but I returned to my faith with a renewed commitment to follow God's ways. Just as today's reading says, God has compassion on us and satisfies us with unfailing love. His favour rests upon us. My wife spent countless hours praying for me as I returned to my faith, and now we pray together for others. Hurt, pain, failure and pride can harden our hearts, but prayer and gentle words of witness can plant the seed of God's love in those who need it most.

Prayer: *Almighty God, thank you for your unfailing love. Help us to plant the seeds of your love so that others may come to know you. Amen*

Thought for the day: How can I plant seeds of God's love today?

Gale A. Richards (Iowa, US)

FRIDAY 17 MARCH

The Power of Prayer

Read Mark 7:24–30

[The woman] begged Jesus to drive the demon out of her daughter.
Mark 7:26 (NIV)

Seventy years ago, at the age of two, I lay strapped to a board for several months. This was the only form of medical help available to those who had infantile paralysis, or polio. Even though the doctor gave me little hope of walking, my mother's faithfulness and relentless prayer life helped to restore my health.

Mark 7:24–30 reminds me how faithful the woman was whose daughter was possessed by a demon. Not only did she beg Jesus for healing, but she was persistent. The grateful mother returned to her home to find her daughter well and everything in good order.

I am inspired by the examples of these two women—my mother and the Syro-Phoenician woman—who were persistent and strong in their faith. God yearns for us to seek strength through prayer as we encounter difficulties and joys. I realise that God loves each of us, no matter how our situation turns out. We, in turn, can express our gratitude for God's strength and presence with us.

Prayer: *Dear Lord, thank you for your constant presence in our lives. Help us to lean on you for strength and guidance. Amen*

Thought for the day: How can I be more faithful in my prayer life?

Lynda S. Phillips (Tennessee, US)

PRAYER FOCUS: PEOPLE WITH POLIO

SATURDAY 18 MARCH

Ready to Serve

Read Philippians 2:12–16
It is God who works in you to will and to act in order to fulfil his good purpose.
Philippians 2:13 (NIV)

When I read the announcement asking for Sunday school teachers, I thought, I want to serve in the church, but I don't feel prepared. I talked with the minister, who encouraged me to give it a try. 'Our children need to hear the word of God,' he said. I accepted the challenge even though I doubted my ability.

On the first Sunday I was to teach the class, I arrived with my own two children. Before the class started, I took a moment to pray at the altar: 'Lord, if only two more children turn up today, I'll know I'm on the right path.' Ten children came that Sunday!

Three years have passed since that first Sunday. Today I have 30 children in the class. They call me 'Teach'. They are generous with hugs and bring me flowers. When I think of how fortunate I am to be involved in God's work, I am overcome with joy. The children's energy enlivens my spiritual life. My ministry has been a welcome oasis in the desert places I have experienced in my life. God graciously prepares each of us in unique ways to serve in just the right ministry.

Prayer: *Loving God, create in each of us a willing heart to follow our path of service to you. Amen*

Thought for the day: Today I will search for opportunities to use my gifts in God's service.

Altagracia Mota Fariña (Dominican Republic)

SUNDAY 19 MARCH

Third Sunday in Lent

Read Matthew 20:29–34

Jesus stood still and called them, saying, 'What do you want me to do for you?'
Matthew 20:32 (NRSV)

When I'm at a social gathering and someone discovers I'm an ordained minister, the person often responds with nervous laughter and says something like, 'I'd better watch my language!' Then sometimes people ask, 'What do I call you? Pastor? Reverend?' They need to know if there's a pattern or some sort of etiquette they need to follow.

At our church, we meet a lot of people who are new to faith, and they often have similar questions about prayer. Is there a pattern to use? A system? Will God be mad if I don't say it correctly? That's one reason I find today's reading so helpful. Jesus asks the two men, 'What do you want me to do for you?' Jesus wants to know their needs and desires. After calling out for mercy, the men say, 'Let our eyes be opened.'

This is a good model for our own prayers. Imagine Jesus asking you, 'What do you want me to do for you?' Christ wants to know our deep desires and then to open our eyes to see where he is present in our lives. When we are not overly concerned with how we pray, we can speak from our hearts and receive Christ's abundant mercy.

Prayer: *Dear Lord of life, show us your mercy and help us to see how deeply you love us. Lead us into a closer relationship with you. Amen*

Thought for the day: I can be honest in my prayers.

Christian Coon (Illinois, US)

PRAYER FOCUS: NEW PEOPLE AT MY CHURCH

MONDAY 20 MARCH

The Discipline of Patience

Read Psalm 130
I wait for the Lord, my whole being waits, and in his word I put my hope
Psalm 130:5 (NIV)

It was raining and I didn't have an umbrella. The bus shelter was full. I was getting wet. I was late. I felt frustrated.

Everyone in the queue was looking at their watches, huffing and puffing and frowning. Some started complaining aloud to the person next to them about the lateness of the bus. One man decided not to wait any more and stomped off to find a taxi.

It's a fact of life that buses are often late. In fact, in this life we have to wait for all kinds of things: exam results, hospital appointments, healing, reconciliation or answers to prayer. We don't like it when our prayers do not appear to be answered or when we have to wait for God to act. Sometimes we complain to him or to others about how long we have to wait. Or we just give up and try to work things out for ourselves.

Perhaps instead, we could practise our 'my whole being waits' skills, both on trivial events like a late bus and more important things, like answers to prayer. In this way we can learn the discipline of patience, cultivating a quiet, trusting heart that is content to wait on the Lord.

Prayer: *Lord, when we find waiting difficult, help us to do so with the right attitude, patiently trusting in you. Amen*

Thought for the day: Today I will practise the discipline of patience.

Fiona Massie (Oxfordshire, UK)

PRAYER FOCUS: BUS DRIVERS

TUESDAY 21 MARCH

The Shadow of Lent

Read Genesis 7:11–24

God said, 'Whenever the rainbow appears in the clouds, I will see it and remember the everlasting covenant between God and all living creatures of every kind on the earth.'
Genesis 9:16 (NIV)

From the large picture window of my childhood home we could watch storms develop across the vast fields. They started as a cloud on the horizon that grew larger and darker as it moved toward us. Lightning and thunder began in the distance, followed by the stirring of the wind and scattering of the birds. Finally, the deep shadow of the storm with its lashing wind and rain arrived. When the storm ended, the sun came out and sometimes a rainbow appeared. I was always amazed by how clear the air was and how clean the earth smelled after the storm. For me, Lent is like the approaching storms of my youth—dark and ominous at the beginning and brighter after it is over.

Lent forces us to look inward. It is a time of silence to listen for God, to read scripture deeply, to pray with compassion for the world. These Lenten disciplines can be challenging, but they reveal insights into the transforming power of the Holy Spirit. Whenever we engage in these practices, our faith can be renewed for the fresh start that will surely follow.

Prayer: *Loving God, help us to focus on the disciplines that strengthen our faith throughout this season, knowing that they will refresh and renew our spirits. Amen*

Thought for the day: Lenten disciplines can help me renew my faith.

F. Richard Garland (Rhode Island, US)

PRAYER FOCUS: SOMEONE EMBRACING A NEW LENTEN PRACTICE

WEDNESDAY 22 MARCH

Strength in Christ

Read Philippians 4:10–13

I can do all things through Christ which strengtheneth me.
Philippians 4:13 (KJV)

For many months, my six children and I were homeless and living in our rundown car. We got most of our food out of rubbish bins. Each day we fought to survive. Family and friends turned away from us as if we had committed a crime. Most people who saw us living in the car pretended they had not seen us. I felt invisible. Everything we owned had been sold as I tried to avoid being homeless. All that was left were some clothes, blankets, some dishes and my Bible.

At night, while the children slept, I cried, not knowing what to do. I prayed, telling God that I was ready to give up. One night I opened my Bible seeking strength and found the verse quoted above. I stared at the words and then read them over and over again, seeing the meaning and the power behind them. This verse assured me that no matter what hardships we face, no matter what obstacles life throws at us, God, through Christ, has given us the strength to overcome them.

From time to time, we all face events that knock us down. They seem too powerful for us to conquer until we remember that we are in God's hands at all times. With the help of God and some loving people he sent to us, my family escaped having to live in the car. I know now that we face nothing alone because through Christ, we fight no battle without God's help.

Prayer: *Thank you, God, for giving us the strength to overcome the challenges of our lives. Amen*

Thought for the day: God will strengthen me and lift me up.

Judy Ann Eichstedt (Oklahoma, US)

PRAYER FOCUS: THOSE WHO ARE HOMELESS

THURSDAY 23 MARCH

No Need for a Monument

Read Genesis 1:1—2:3
[God's] glory covered the heavens and his praise filled the earth.
Habakkuk 3:3 (NIV)

On 23 March 2015, the founding prime minister of Singapore, Mr Lee Kuan Yew, passed away. He is considered the father of modern Singapore because he led the growth of the small nation from a lowly outpost into a developed country. When he died, many people wondered how to honour him. A physical monument or towering edifice for Mr Lee was considered. But many people commented, 'Look around Singapore, and you will see and remember his legacy.' Their comments reminded me of Genesis 1:1: 'In the beginning God created the heavens and the earth.'

As we look around us, at the sky, the sea, the land, we see the wonderful creation of our great God. Psalm 19:1 says, 'The heavens declare the glory of God; the skies proclaim the work of his hands.' Our intricate bodies are also a testament to God's work.

Psalm 139:13–14 says, 'You created my inmost being; you knit me together in my mother's womb. I praise you because I am fearfully and wonderfully made; your works are wonderful, I know that full well.'

God needs no monument to declare his greatness. Creation and the Lord's handiwork are there for all to see. From creation, we know that God is the Almighty One, who is ever-present and loves and protects us with power and grace.

Prayer: *Heavenly Father, thank you for your creation. Protect us and guide us to honour and glorify you always. Amen*

Thought for the day: Where in creation do I see God's greatness?

Kong Peng Sun (Singapore)

PRAYER FOCUS: WORLD LEADERS

FRIDAY 24 MARCH

A Cup of Tea

Read Matthew 25:35–40

Jesus said, 'Truly I tell you, anyone who gives you a cup of water in my name because you belong to the Messiah will certainly not lose their reward.'
Mark 9:41 (NIV)

It was a dry, dusty afternoon. Spring was turning to summer in Italy, and the smell of the sea drifted from the port and wound through the narrow streets. Difficult circumstances in my life as an exchange student were overwhelming me.

That day, after months of trying to cope, I fell apart. As I walked home, my eyes were so full of tears I could barely see, so I sat down on a step. I'm not sure how long I sat there before I heard a voice. I looked up, startled, to see a woman calling to me from her window across the street. She asked again, 'Excuse me, Miss. Would you like some tea? A cup of tea will do you good.' A few moments later she arrived with a cup, saucer, tea bag, spoon and kettle. She poured the water for me, offered me milk and sugar, and disappeared, saying only that I could leave the cup there when I had finished.

Years later, I don't remember exactly why I was crying, but I remember that cup of tea and the woman's kindness. Her hospitality was like that of the people in today's reading who unknowingly served the Lord by serving others. How often do we take time to show hospitality to strangers? Nothing could be more important.

Prayer: *Loving God, show us how we can extend your kindness to someone who needs it today, and help us to recognise you in those who are in pain. In Jesus' name. Amen*

Thought for the day: When I show kindness to others I show kindness to Christ.

Hannah Kallio (Minnesota, US)

PRAYER FOCUS: EXCHANGE STUDENTS

SATURDAY 25 MARCH

'Thank You For Being Here'

Read Psalm 118:5–14
O give thanks to the Lord, call on his name, make known his deeds among the peoples.
1 Chronicles 16:8 (NRSV)

As a public utility worker for many years, I went out on service calls—often at odd times and to bad situations. Many times, I was greeted by someone who acted as if I were personally responsible for the sudden disruption. I was often accused of being incompetent, irresponsible and even sometimes of causing the problem in order to get overtime pay. Such words hardened my heart and caused me to have bad feelings about others. But usually at least one person in every situation would say, 'Thank you for being here.' Those words of gratitude always outweighed whatever bad things others might have said.

We all have experienced sudden disruptions in our lives—the kind that no call to an ordinary worker could fix. In these moments we need help that only the Lord can provide. And we can trust that when we call to God in prayer, no matter the time or place, he will come and restore us. And to God we can always say, 'Thank you for being here.'

Prayer: *O holy Father, never let us forget that when we call on you in faith, you will be there to give us strength. As Jesus taught us, we pray, 'Father, hallowed be your name, your kingdom come. Give us each day our daily bread. Forgive us our sins, for we also forgive everyone who sins against us. And lead us not into temptation.'* Amen*

Thought for the day: God is always on call for me.

Mark A. Carter (Texas, US)

PRAYER FOCUS: PUBLIC UTILITY WORKERS
* Luke 11:2–4, NIV

SUNDAY 26 MARCH

Fourth Sunday in Lent

Read Luke 5:12–16

[Jesus] said to [his disciples], 'When you pray, say: Father, hallowed be your name. Your kingdom come.'
Luke 11:2 (NRSV)

My daughter Alexis is an active three-year-old who loves to talk. Her favourite question is, 'Why?' Many days we have in-depth conversations about why I go to work, why she goes to school, and even why we have to sleep at night.

Recently she asked, 'Why do we pray?' I paused to think. After a few moments of silence, I simply responded, 'To remind us that God is with us.' Alexis paused before asking, 'Where does God live?' I admire her inquisitiveness.

The disciples who followed Jesus were also inquisitive and asked Jesus how they should pray. Jesus' response in Luke 11 is not simply a pattern to be repeated but rather a call to relationship. Jesus reminds us that prayer is not about perfect words, but rather a heart inclined toward God. Prayer fosters an inner peace that enables us to persevere even when we can't answer every 'why' question. It develops trust that God will provide all that we need and reminds us that forgiveness is a daily gift. Prayer shapes a desire for God's kingdom rather than our own.

Prayer: *Dear God, give us the strength and power, through your Holy Spirit, to trust you to transform the world and to transform us. Let thy will be done. Amen*

Thought for the day: In times of uncertainty, I will pray to God.

Lia McIntosh (Missouri, US)

MONDAY 27 MARCH

Tunnels

Read 2 Corinthians 4:17–18

Do not fear, for I am with you, do not be afraid, for I am your God; I will strengthen you, I will help you, I will uphold you with my victorious right hand.
Isaiah 41:10 (NRSV)

A few years ago our family was returning from a road trip to Mumbai. I was driving on Mumbai–Pune Expressway and enjoying the scenic stretch surrounded by hills and valleys. Suddenly, though, we entered a tunnel.

Closed spaces make me nervous and dizzy, as though I am going to be swallowed by the darkness. So fear gripped me the moment I realised I was driving through a tunnel. I was so nervous that I could not breathe. I wanted to stop the car and allow my husband to drive, but it was too dangerous to stop the car.

Seeing my worry, my husband and children were quick to point out the speck of light that indicated that the tunnel was going to end soon. I started focusing on the light, and I began to feel better. Before I knew it, I was out of the tunnel and felt as if I could breathe freely again.

Sometimes in life we find ourselves in dark, tunnel-like situations that leave us terrified and exhausted. When we hold strong to our faith, God can guide us out of our troubles by giving us a speck of light to focus on. Ultimately, these experiences make us stronger emotionally and spiritually.

Prayer: *Dear Guide of humanity, help us to remember that our strength lies in you. We pray in Jesus' name. Amen*

Thought for the day: God is with me in my struggles today.

Sahana Mathias (Karnataka, India)

PRAYER FOCUS: SOMEONE STRUGGLING WITH ANXIETY

TUESDAY 28 MARCH

Lessons of Love

Read 1 John 4:7–12

Beloved, since God loved us so much, we also ought to love one another.
1 John 4:11 (NRSV)

My 87-year-old father enjoys feeding the birds. One day, I was visiting him after he had thrown food out for them. Instead of attracting the normal small birds that live around his house, the food attracted a large number of loud, annoying crows. I complained to my dad about throwing out food and attracting crows to the house. His answer was short and to the point: 'Even the crows have to eat.'

I learned a valuable lesson that day. Sometimes, when I am trying to help someone who is being difficult, I remember my father's words. Many people in my life are lovable; but deep down, I know that people who are not easy to love deserve the same care. Jesus taught us that love is not always easy.

My dad understands that one day a birdfeeder will bring him the joy of seeing a colourful goldfinch. And then when he least expects it, along come noisy crows to squabble over and scoop up the food. His love for the birds is like God's love for us: benevolent and unconditional.

Prayer: *Heavenly Father, guide our hearts so that our love for others reflects your love. Thank you for people who show us how to be your loving followers. Amen*

Thought for the day: I will abide in God's love.

Patricia Lucksavage (Tennessee, US)

PRAYER FOCUS: WILDLIFE

WEDNESDAY 29 MARCH

A Party With Presents

Read Acts 20:32–35
Give, and it will be given to you. A good measure, pressed down, shaken together, running over, will be put into your lap; for the measure you give will be the measure you get back.
Luke 6:38 (NRSV)

When asked what he wanted for his fifth birthday party, my grandson Caleb said, 'A party with presents. Everybody brings a present, and then we will take all the presents to the homeless shelter for the children who don't have anything for their birthdays.' And that is exactly what they did. Caleb said it was the most fun he had ever had on his birthday.

Jesus reminds us to give. When we give out of a generous and loving spirit, a 'good measure' will come to us. That good measure can come to us as a sense of joy and satisfaction when we show love to others. When we acknowledge that we have learned something about sharing and live out that lesson, when we give expecting nothing in return, God can take our gifts and use them to offer someone else abundant life. Good measure comes when we realise that giving from the heart has its own reward.

Prayer: *Give us generous hearts, minds and spirits, O God, so that what we give may help others to know your love. Through Jesus Christ, we pray. Amen*

Thought for the day: How can I use my gifts to bless others?

John B. Tate, Jr (Washington, DC, US)

PRAYER FOCUS: CHILDREN WHO ARE HOMELESS

THURSDAY 30 MARCH

God Is Trustworthy

Read Luke 14:25–27

Trust in the Lord with all your heart and lean not on your own understanding; in all your ways submit to him, and he will make your paths straight.
Proverbs 3:5–6 (NIV)

I thought I was settled for life. Bob and I had graduated from college, married and were living in our home town. Then, God called my husband to full-time ministry. Pulled up by my roots, I realised that the journey ahead would not be easy. In the past, trust, obedience and risk had been only words to me. I had wanted to love and serve God, yet also remain in control of my life. I had never taken seriously the words of Jesus, 'Anyone who loves their father or mother more than me is not worthy of me; anyone who loves their son or daughter more than me is not worthy of me' (Matthew 10:37).

Through earnest prayer and study of the scriptures, I began a soul-searching journey, discovering how to trust and obey God's will for my life. Trust is a process of giving ourselves to God, believing that he is trustworthy. It leads to the realisation that every step we take is guided by the one who already knows our path and who will lead us to our identity as children of God.

Prayer: *Dear Lord, thank you for people who are willing to give up everything to serve you. Help us to trust you and to be obedient to your call on our lives. Amen*

Thought for the day: Putting my trust in God takes practice.

Carole J. Murphy (Georgia, US)

FRIDAY 31 MARCH

Guidance and Hope

Read Psalm 25:1–10

Show me your ways, Lord, teach me your paths. Guide me in your truth and teach me, for you are God my Saviour, and my hope is in you all day long.
Psalm 25:4–5 (NIV)

Every day I ask for God's guidance. I share my problems and concerns with God and place them in his hands. But as I write this meditation, it is difficult. I am holding back tears knowing that all employees at my place of work—people whom I have loved and valued for the past eight years—will be laid off, and we will no longer be working side by side. Today I can't think clearly because my sadness is clouding my perception. However, I do count on God and trust that he will console me in the days ahead.

The author of Proverbs encourages us to trust God with all our hearts, not to lean on our own understanding, and assures us that God will lead us in the right path (Proverbs 3:5–6). What God said to Jeremiah is also valid for us today. God knows our every thought and when we call, he will listen (see Jeremiah 29:11–14).

Uncertainty can be troubling. However, we can hold fast to the words found in Deuteronomy 31:8: 'The Lord himself goes before you and will be with you; he will never leave you nor forsake you. Do not be afraid; do not be discouraged.'

Prayer: *Loving God, shine your light to guide our path. Help us not to waver in our faith but remain steadfast. Amen*

Thought for the day: In uncertain circumstances, God will remain steadfast.

Yanisse González (Puerto Rico)

PRAYER FOCUS: SOMEONE WHO HAS LOST A JOB

SATURDAY 1 APRIL

Remember Me?

Read Isaiah 43:1–4

Now, says the Lord—the one who created you, Jacob, the one who formed you, Israel: Don't fear, for I have redeemed you; I have called you by name; you are mine.
Isaiah 43:1 (CEB)

My husband and I are retired teachers. Sometimes we are approached by former students who ask, 'Do you remember me?' Most of the time we can recall their names. Sometimes not; after all, we have not seen them for years, and we have known thousands of children over our careers.

A look of sadness or disappointment often crosses the student's face when we fail to recall a name, and we feel bad about it. On occasions when we do remember a student's name, we see joy on the person's face and a twinkle in his or her eyes. Usually, we talk about classroom memories. The students' faces reveal that being known and remembered is good.

What I find most remarkable is that God never forgets any of us. Though each of us is only one among billions, he always knows who we are. No matter how far we stray or how much time passes before we return to the Lord, God always remembers us, loves us and calls us by name.

Prayer: *Creator God, thank you for knowing us fully and loving us completely. Amen*

Thought for the day: God will always remember me.

Janet Holloway-Bergman (Missouri, US)

PRAYER FOCUS: TEACHERS AND STUDENTS

SUNDAY 2 APRIL

Fifth Sunday in Lent

Read Mark 9:43–48

If your hand causes you to stumble, cut it off.
Mark 9:43 (NIV)

There are over 60 languages spoken in my neighbourhood, making it one of the most diverse communities in the world. The beauty of our diversity is tainted by a long history of discrimination. Tensions are particularly high between our mostly white police force and our African and African-American populations.

Recently, our church helped to organise a local community clean up. As we picked up litter together, I asked an officer, 'What is your number one priority?' and was delighted when he said, 'Creating positive relations between the police force and the community.' I asked how we could help him to right the wrongs of the past and move forward in this new direction. I was deeply disappointed when he explained that he saw no problem with the past and simply wanted everyone to get along going forward. In that moment I realised my own shallow view of repentance. Like the officer, I often want a fruitful future without confronting the sin of my past.

In Mark 9, Jesus teaches us that repentance is more than simply apologising. When Jesus uses the image of cutting off a part of ourselves where sin has made a home, I hear him saying that true repentance requires us to confront our past sin and to make a change. Jesus' grace brings new life to each of us and also to our communities.

Prayer: *Gracious God, grant us the courage to confront the sin in our lives and in our communities. Give us the strength to change ourselves and our world for the better. Amen*

Thought for the day: God's transforming grace is always available to me.

John Helmiere (Washington, US)

PRAYER FOCUS: LEADERS IN MY COMMUNITY

MONDAY 3 APRIL

Where Are You, God?

Read Psalm 22:1–5

My God, why have you forsaken me?
Psalm 22:1 (NIV)

The words of David in Psalm 22 are echoed by Jesus from the cross. It is a cry that shares our own distress when we sense that God has abandoned us in our trouble or tragedy, and we need to hear from him. 'Why?' we ask, and yet it seems that God doesn't answer. Difficulties come uninvited and are unwelcome: personal loss, injustice, or ill health and ageing. Our experience is individual and isolating, and often others neither understand nor can they truly enter our sorrow or pain. These experiences strip us of the frivolous and take us to the core of who we are.

And in that place, I've found I have a choice. I can journey into God and connect with him in a deeper way. I can choose to let go of my tendency to be self-sufficient and trust his all-embracing sufficiency. This wilderness of the soul doesn't have to be desolate. God hasn't answered my 'Why' but he answers by affirming his presence with me. I've discovered that God walks with me through the pain and heartache.

In this psalm David rehearses the faith of us all—God is to be trusted. He will not disappoint us. I know that God will not let my foot or your foot slip. Ever.

Prayer: *Father God, you promise to be with us, always. Thank you that I can trust you whatever happens. Amen*

Thought for the day: I will remember God's presence with me today.

Hilary Allen (Somerset, UK)

TUESDAY 4 APRIL

Strong and Courageous

Read Joshua 1:1–9

Keep alert, stand firm in your faith, be courageous, be strong. Let all that you do be done in love.
1 Corinthians 16:13–14 (NRSV)

While praying for a new church home, my family met two other families who were praying for the same thing. Together we formed a house church. We met for worship and fellowship on Tuesdays and Sundays. We read the Bible and communicated daily. But now, other obligations were taking one family away. This was our last fellowship before they departed. 'We will miss you,' I said, clearing a lump from my throat. My spirit sagged.

We read Joshua 1:1–9. Joshua faced both the death of Moses and leaving the land he had known. Joshua had been Moses' young assistant, and Moses had encouraged and strengthened Joshua, commissioning him to lead the Israelites into the promised land (Deuteronomy 3:28). God's advice to Joshua to sustain him was straightforward, 'Be strong and courageous' (Joshua 1:6). 'As I was with Moses, so I will be with you; I will not fail you or forsake you' (Joshua 1:5). Like Joshua, I drew courage and strength from God's promise. He would be with us and with our departing friends.

Prayer: *Thank you, God, for the gift of fellowship with other believers. Grant us the courage and strength to love one another. Amen*

Thought for the day: Christian fellowship is a gift from God.

C. Stephen Smith (Texas, US)

PRAYER FOCUS: HOUSE CHURCHES

WEDNESDAY 5 APRIL

Leftovers

Read Deuteronomy 26:1–10
God is able to provide you with every blessing in abundance, so that by always having enough of everything, you may share abundantly in every good work.
2 Corinthians 9:8 (NRSV)

I often serve my family leftovers to save myself a little time. The original meal is usually delicious. But when I serve the leftovers several days later I sometimes feel that I haven't given my best.

I sometimes serve myself spiritual leftovers as well. I fit God in, instead of making time with him my first priority. I say a quick thank you to God each morning instead of taking time throughout the day to appreciate the opportunities he offers me. I neglect to read God's word each day. Just as physical food nourishes our bodies, God's word is meant to feed our souls, and we are invited to receive it afresh each day.

I serve God leftovers too. I follow my own will first and consider his will as an afterthought—or after my way hasn't worked out. God instructed the Israelites to give their first-fruits as an acknowledgement that every blessing comes from him. When we give God our first-fruits, we acknowledge that he is sovereign over us. Such awareness helps us to keep alive the excitement of having God in our lives and gives us the courage to do his will.

Prayer: *O God, may we seek you and your kingdom first and not become too busy to give you our best. Amen*

Thought for the day: I'm never too busy to spend time with God.

Jean Bonin (Alberta, Canada)

THURSDAY 6 APRIL

My Worst Day

Read Isaiah 6:1–10
'I'm here; send me.'
Isaiah 6:8 (CEB)

On the worst day of my mission work in Africa, I woke up early to drive several hours into the bush. I got lost multiple times before finally finding the church where I was scheduled to teach. Even though I was late, I waited several hours while the congregation slowly gathered and sang songs under the shade of a large tree. When I eventually spoke to the group, the lesson I had prepared fell apart. The crowd looked bored, and I wondered whether the translation of my message was clear. When I finally got home that night, I cried myself to sleep, thinking, 'Lord, what am I doing here?'

Several weeks later, I went back to the same village. One of the women on my team was talking with a local man. 'I am a Christian,' he said. 'Wonderful!' she replied, 'How long have you been a Christian?' 'Three weeks,' he answered. 'Really?' she asked, 'How did you become a Christian?' The man shifted his weight against his walking stick and lifted his arm to point at me as I entered the camp, 'That man came.'

On what I felt was my worst day, I learned the lesson of Isaiah 6:8. My success or failure as a follower of God has little to do with my abilities and everything to do with my availability. The harvest is up to God; Jesus simply invited me to help scatter the seed (see Mark 4:26–29).

Prayer: *Dear Lord, help us to remember that faithfulness is more important than 'success' and our availability is more important than our abilities. Amen*

Thought for the day: Success is being available to share the word of God.

Bryan Brigham (Texas, US)

PRAYER FOCUS: NEW BELIEVERS

FRIDAY 7 APRIL

Pray a Happy Prayer

Read 1 Thessalonians 5:16–18
Rejoice in the Lord always. I will say it again: Rejoice!
Philippians 4:4 (NIV)

As my daughter neared the end of her long and difficult battle with cancer, her husband and her father and I were often at her bedside. I'm sure our prayers reflected the sadness we felt, anticipating the separation we knew was coming. But one day our daughter said, 'Mum, pray a happy prayer.' I immediately understood. She wanted to hear a prayer that was not about her illness, but a prayer thanking God for our family's love, the happy years we'd had together, and our faith that we would be united in our heavenly home.

With her request, my prayer life was forever changed. From that day forward, I have tried to pray joyful prayers. God loves us, and Jesus died for our sins and has prepared a glorious home in heaven for us—ample reason to rejoice.

Of course, some sadness is inevitable. Even Jesus wept when his friend Lazarus died. But I will always be thankful to my beloved daughter for asking me to pray a happy prayer. Words like rejoice, glad and joy abound in the Bible. And I can't help but believe that God is pleased with prayers of praise and thanksgiving.

Prayer: *Dear God, we praise you for your mercy and grace. Help us to understand that you are the source of true happiness in our lives. Amen*

Thought for the day: I will pray a 'happy prayer' today.

Peggy Orr Mason (Tennessee, US)

PRAYER FOCUS: GRIEVING PARENTS

SATURDAY 8 APRIL

The Peace of God

Read Isaiah 26:1–9

You will keep in perfect peace those whose minds are steadfast, because they trust in you.
Isaiah 26:3 (NIV)

A few months ago I flew in a small plane. As the plane moved down the runway and began to gain altitude, I noticed the change in cabin pressure. Feeling slightly fearful, I started to pray: 'Please, no turbulence. May this be a peaceful flight.'

Life can be like this plane ride, with unexpected events and surprises: a grave illness, the sudden death of a loved one or the loss of a job. These events are the 'turbulence' we encounter in our lives.

It is amazing to know that despite the turbulence, God is always with us, in the centre of every circumstance, and provides the peace that surpasses all understanding. When we draw close to God and ask for help, we can be reminded that Christ is always with us, 'to the very end of the age' (Matthew 28:20).

Prayer: *Loving God, thank you for your constant presence among us. Grant us your peace that surpasses all understanding. We pray as Jesus taught us, saying, 'Our Father in heaven, hallowed be your name, your kingdom come, your will be done on earth as it is in heaven. Give us today our daily bread. Forgive us our debts, as we also have forgiven our debtors. And lead us not into temptation, but deliver us from the evil one.'* Amen*

Thought for the day: When I trust in God, I can find peace.

Ma Magdalena Alvarado G. (Coahuila, Mexico)

PRAYER FOCUS: PILOTS
* Matthew 6:9–13, NIV

SUNDAY 9 APRIL

Palm Sunday

Read Luke 23:23–42
Let us run with perseverance the race marked out for us.
Hebrews 12:1 (NIV)

For ten years my husband has participated in international triathlon events called Ironman. People from all over the world gather to complete a journey of 140.6 miles. They have 17 hours to swim 2.4 miles, cycle 112 miles and run 26.2 miles. Though the best athletes in the world take part in this event, it is not just for star performers. Ironman is for anyone who dares and desires to train and test his or her physical and emotional endurance. At the core, Ironman is a journey of perseverance.

Perseverance is an attribute that scripture honours and Jesus exemplified. His ministry and journey to the cross is the epitome of grace wrapped in courage. He knew the course set before him and the goal. He knew he had the Father's love to strengthen him. When we face challenging parts of our journeys, we can look to Christ. He understands what a difficult road looks like and knows what it means to keep going. God gives us strength to persevere.

Prayer: *Dear Jesus, by your example and in your strength, help us to persevere through the trials that come our way. Amen*

Thought for the day: Today I will follow Jesus' example of perseverance.

Kimberly MacNeill (Tennessee, US)

PRAYER FOCUS: SOMEONE FACING DIFFICULTIES

MONDAY 10 APRIL

Strength from God

Read Isaiah 61:1–3

Say hello to Andronicus and Junia, my relatives and my fellow prisoners. They are prominent among the apostles, and they were in Christ before me.

Romans 16:7 (CEB)

As a part of my personal ministry, I volunteer at a local prison, and I am humbled to be around the men of F Block. Many of the men there have lost almost everything: their families, their jobs, their homes and their reputations. But they have not lost the love of our Lord and Saviour Jesus Christ. Their faith in God is unquenchable. They know that through the love of God they can turn their lives around and become the men they believe God wants them to be.

I always ask each man his prayer requests and almost all of them ask for the Lord to continue to strengthen their faith. They pray to be like the Apostle Paul who found strength from God while in prison.

I used to hope that my visits would bless those who are incarcerated. But this ministry has richly blessed me as well. Seeing the undying love for God and strong faith in Jesus Christ among men who have lost so much is the greatest testimony to the transformative power of God I have ever witnessed. Thanks to the men of F Block, I have become stronger in my faith.

Prayer: *Dear Lord, bless the men and women who are imprisoned. Strengthen and sustain their faith and ours. Amen*

Thought for the day: How has God strengthened my faith through the faith of another?

Dave Shiple (South Carolina, US)

PRAYER FOCUS: THOSE WHO ARE IN PRISON

TUESDAY 11 APRIL

Testing the Pond

Read Mark 10:46–52
Those who know your name trust in you, for you, Lord, have never forsaken those who seek you.
Psalm 9:10 (NIV)

Growing up, my brothers and I loved to skate and play hockey on the frozen pond near our house. Finding out when it was solid enough to skate on was quite a process. When the temperature began to drop, we would wrap up and visit the pond to check the progress. To measure the thickness of the ice, we did everything from poking through the edge of the ice to throwing large rocks toward the middle to see if they would fall through. When the rocks would glide across the pond, we deemed it safe enough for my older brother to test it. As my younger brother and I watched anxiously on the edge ready to rescue him, he would venture out. Sometimes the ice would creak from his weight and he would retreat. But when it didn't, we were elated because we knew the pond was ready for skating.

For me, trusting God has been similar to my pond experience. Even though I know that God, like the solid ice, can bear the weight of my burdens, I can still be tentative about transferring them. I have to remind myself that Jesus Christ has gone before me and shown me that it is safe to rely on God. Not only is it safe, but also it can be liberating and even exhilarating!

Prayer: *Dear steadfast and loving God, trusting you doesn't always come easily. Please forgive us when we doubt and help us to trust you. Amen*

Thought for the day: God can handle the weight of my burdens.

Gail Fritz (North Carolina, US)

WEDNESDAY 12 APRIL

The Path of Mercy

Read Luke 10:25–37

'Which of these three… was a neighbour to the man who fell into the hands of the robbers?' [Jesus asked]. He said, 'The one who showed him mercy.'
Luke 10:36–37 (NRSV)

Many people know the story of the good Samaritan and his compassion for the man who was in crisis. I find it interesting that the verb in today's quoted verse is 'showed'. It doesn't say 'the one who spoke about mercy' but rather the one who actively 'showed him mercy'. The Samaritan demonstrated his mercy by stopping his own journey, binding up the man's wounds, transporting him to safety and providing money so that his care would continue after he left. The Samaritan also returned and visited the man once his journey obligations were finished.

The good Samaritan did not just pat the man on the head, pray over him and then go on his way. He devoted significant time and effort and, as he was someone who was considered an outcast, his involvement cost him time, money and personal risk. Jesus told the story to teach us what being a neighbour means and what a neighbour does, even when—or especially when—it calls for great sacrifice.

Prayer: *Heavenly Father, teach us to be good neighbours, and guide us as we show compassion to others. Amen*

Thought for the day: To whom can I show God's mercy today?

Virginia Ruth (Maryland, US)

PRAYER FOCUS: FOR A MORE COMPASSIONATE SOCIETY

THURSDAY 13 APRIL

A Secure Grip

Read John 15:4–8

Jesus said, 'On that day you will realise that I am in the Father, and you are in me, and I am in you.'
John 14:20 (NIV)

When I was young, my family went walking in the forests of Hogsback, in the Eastern Cape of South Africa. To get to the top of the slope, we first had to scramble up a steep muddy path next to a big waterfall. My dad suggested that we should hold hands to keep me from sliding down the slope. Instead of actually holding hands, he held my wrist and had me hold on to his wrist. That way if one of us should stumble and let go, the other would still be holding fast. This gave me a sense of security as we climbed the steep slope.

Like my dad, Jesus wanted to reassure his disciples. The night before his crucifixion, he warned them that he would be leaving.

However, he also promised that he would return, assuring them that death could not hold him. He spoke of the relationship his disciples would have with him and the Father through the Spirit.

Jesus still reaches out to us today. As our reading for today tells us, if we remain in Jesus, we will have the joy of bearing much fruit for him (see John 15:4–8). His promise is our assurance that he will remain in us. Even if we stumble, Jesus will not let go.

Prayer: *Dear Lord Jesus, help us to remain in you throughout this day, walking in love, joy and obedience. Amen*

Thought for the day: My obedience to Jesus brings glory to God.

John McCutcheon (Limpopo, South Africa)

FRIDAY 14 APRIL

Good Friday

Read John 15:9–17

Jesus replied [to Andrew and Philip], 'Very truly I tell you, unless a kernel of wheat falls to the ground and dies, it remains only a single seed. But if it dies, it produces many seeds.'
John 12:24 (NIV)

Each year when my husband and I plant corn, we marvel as the kernels we plant grow and become stalks with many ears of corn, each ear with many kernels on it. It is something we can depend on. Jesus taught about this principle after his triumphal entry into Jerusalem, in the week before his death, burial and resurrection.

Using the illustration quoted above, he prepared his followers to accept that he would have to die and be buried so that they and many others might have new life. Rather than warning his followers to guard their lives, Jesus encouraged them to be willing to lose them. The willingness to lose their lives freed them to abandon their own interests and devote themselves to ministry. Jesus would soon charge them to go into the whole world, teaching and living by Jesus' example. And Jesus challenges us to do the same.

Prayer: *Thank you, Jesus, for showing your undying love for us by dying for our sins. Amen*

Thought for the day: What am I willing to lose so that others might have new life in Christ?

Shirley McCoy (Florida, US)

PRAYER FOCUS: FARMERS

SATURDAY 15 APRIL

To Pray Is to Change

Read Romans 5:3–5

Let each of you look not to your own interests, but to the interests of others.
Philippians 2:4 (NRSV)

Last year I was diagnosed with a deadly heart disease. The prognosis was grim and my sole option was a highly specialised operation. Fortunately, I was judged to be suitable for the surgery. I was scared, and I didn't know if I would return home.

While awaiting surgery, I attended the outpatients' clinic several times for tests. I often saw the same people who were there for the same reason as I was, and came to know some of them quite well.

Day by day my prayers became less focused on me and my illness. I began to look to the needs of the other patients and began praying for them. When one of my new friends died, I helped to console his family. Another patient and I encouraged each other as we went through the various tests and procedures required for our surgery and as we recuperated after our operations.

I prayed for healing, but over the course of my treatment I learned that to pray is to change. God provided an opportunity for me to witness to others, to reassure them and to encourage them. When we trust God and turn our focus to others, we can be changed.

Prayer: *Dear Lord, open our eyes and hearts to your will. Help us to trust you enough so that we can focus on others and not just on ourselves. Amen*

Thought for the day: How has prayer changed me?

Arthur J. Williams, Jr (California, US)

PRAYER FOCUS: THOSE UNDERGOING SURGERY

SUNDAY 16 APRIL

Easter Sunday

Read Luke 24:1–12

When [the women] returned from the tomb, they reported all these things to the eleven and all the others.
Luke 24:9 (CEB)

None of the biblical accounts explain how the resurrection took place. The Gospel writers say nothing about how the stone was rolled away or what happened to bring Jesus back to life. Did his heart just begin beating and the other organs gradually restart? Did the resurrection occur instantly or over a period of several hours?

None of these questions is answered. The scripture simply tells us that people at Jesus' tomb discovered the living among the dead. Perhaps the Bible is telling us something important by leaving out the details: God is at work even when we can't see him in action. God is still doing something when we think he has finished. Most importantly, the Easter story communicates by its lack of detail that we don't have to understand how God works in order for him to work.

The women who went to the tomb on Easter morning expected to find a dead body. They did not expect a miracle but kept living faithfully and demonstrated their devotion. In the process, they experienced renewed hope and ran to share it with others.

Even when we don't feel like it, we can act on our faith, serve others, give generously and worship faithfully. In this way, we put ourselves in a position to experience what God can do, what he is already doing.

Prayer: *Loving God, thank you for the miracle of Easter. Give us the strength to serve others even when it isn't easy. Amen*

Thought for the day: Today I can experience the hope that Jesus' resurrection offers.

Rob Fuquay (Indiana, US)

PRAYER FOCUS: PEOPLE CELEBRATING EASTER AROUND THE WORLD

MONDAY 17 APRIL

The Best out of the Worst

Read Romans 8:28–39
We know that all things work together for good for those who love God, who are called according to his purpose.
Romans 8:28 (NRSV)

Every Easter morning my family would gather at the table to begin our Easter celebration by eating rice bread that our mother baked for us. One Easter morning, my siblings and I were excited to eat the rice bread when we heard a yell coming from the kitchen. We rushed to see what had happened. There stood Mother, holding the bread with the top and bottom burned. We could see the disappointment on her face. While we waited, Mother found a solution. She removed the burned portions and took the rest to the table. As we ate that bread, we realised that it was the best Easter bread Mother had ever baked.

This experience reminds me of Romans 8:28: all things work for the good of those who respond to God in love. I would not have tasted the best of my mother's baking if she had thrown out the burned rice bread. At times, we forget God's promise to turn our worst into the best, our bitterness into sweetness, and our difficult situation into a beautiful one. God can bring the best out of the worst.

Prayer: *Dear all-powerful God, thank you for working for our good in every situation. Amen*

Thought for the day: I can trust God even in unpleasant situations.

George Weagba (Montserrado, Liberia)

PRAYER FOCUS: THOSE WHO HAVE NOTHING TO EAT

TUESDAY 18 APRIL

God's Perfect Harmony

Read 1 Corinthians 12:12–27
Let the peace of Christ rule in your hearts, to which you were called in one body. And be thankful.
Colossians 3:15 (NRSV)

For my birthday one year, my daughter gave me a collection of gospel music. The collection contains nearly everything—classic hymns, artists that my parents grew up listening to and current gospel singers. Sometimes, I have the music playing softly in the background while I write. Or I play it loudly when I do chores around the house. The music brings me countless hours of joy, peace and encouragement.

When I hear the harmonies of music, I think about all the people involved in creating it. It takes an entire team—songwriters, musicians and singers—working together to blend all the different sounds we love to hear. In the same way God wants us to operate in harmony with one another as we work together to help build the kingdom, spreading the message of salvation and eternal life.

We all experience countless ups and downs as we journey through life. When we interact with our brothers and sisters in Christ, reaching out to help one another, we gain strength and courage to persevere. As we learn to support one another, pray for each other and work together, we become the example that Jesus commanded us to be when he said, 'Love one another' (John 13:34).

Prayer: *Dear Lord, show us how to love one another so that the world will be drawn to you. In Jesus' name we pray. Amen*

Thought for the day: God gives us different abilities so we can meet the needs of the world.

Dorothea Love (California, US)

PRAYER FOCUS: PROFESSIONAL MUSICIANS

WEDNESDAY 19 APRIL

Someone Prayed for Me

Read John 17:20–26

Jesus spoke to his Father, 'My prayer is not for them alone. I pray also for those who will believe in me through their message.'
John 17:20 (NIV)

Each time I read the verses of today's scripture reading, I remember a special woman, a servant of God, who prayed for me during a time when I was rebelling against God. I also remember that Jesus prayed for those who would believe in him because they heard the disciples' message. I feel a sense of joy believing that Christ was praying for me even at that moment.

At times we may feel restless or concerned for certain people and feel moved to include them in prayer. The Holy Spirit nudges us and guides us as we pray. We do not need to hesitate to name those people before God, for surely they are in need of intercessory prayer. I am where I am today and have become who I am because a special woman never stopped praying for me—and for many others.

Prayer: *Loving God, thank you for welcoming us with open arms and for the many prayers of intercession offered by those who care about us. Amen*

Thought for the day: My prayers can make a difference in others' lives.

Sandra Cerezo Barth (Santa Fe, Argentina)

PRAYER FOCUS: SOMEONE WHO HAS PRAYED FOR ME

THURSDAY 20 APRIL

The Gift of Laughter

Read Genesis 21:1–7
Sarah said, 'God has brought me laughter, and everyone who hears about this will laugh with me.'
Genesis 21:6 (NIV)

One Sunday morning I noticed many solemn faces in my congregation. I knew these people well, and many concerns weighed on their hearts. As I invited the children to come forward for their special talk, they marched slowly up the centre aisle, peering at all the sad faces. My two-year-old son, Isaac, however, sprinted down the aisle yelling, 'Daddy!' and threw himself into my arms. I looked over at my wife, Isaac's mummy, sitting in the front row, and then noticed that the entire church had erupted in laughter as they responded to Isaac's joyful exclamation.

For years Abraham's wife Sarah wanted a child. She had hoped, prayed and wept sorrowfully. But her suffering was only temporary. Now that this miracle, Isaac, had been born, she laughed—looking forward to sharing the good news with those who would laugh with her.

In this world, we are surrounded by heartaches and serious concerns. However, God is with us and he can still give us joy. Sometimes the joy comes to us directly, as it did for Sarah. Sometimes it comes to us indirectly through the joy of others. However the gift of joy comes, it is a big reminder that the heartaches and concerns of this world are only temporary.

Prayer: *Joyful Creator, help us experience the gift of laughter and help us to rejoice with others. Amen*

Thought for the day: When laughter finds me, I am experiencing God at work.

Geoffrey L. Snook (Kansas, US)

PRAYER FOCUS: SOMEONE WAITING FOR A CHILD

FRIDAY 21 APRIL

The Aroma of Christ

Read Luke 15:11–32

We smell like the aroma of Christ's offering to God, both to those who are being saved and to those who are on the road to destruction.
2 Corinthians 2:15 (CEB)

I used to work at a local mission. Some of my most vivid memories of that place are of the distinct smells I encountered there. Before guests arrived, the aroma of the day's lunch would begin to permeate the air. Then as people came in we greeted them all, many with a hug. Sometimes I would enjoy the fragrances of freshly shampooed hair. Other friends would bring in the distinct smell of having spent the night by an open campfire. Others stood before me with the overpowering odour of stale cigarettes and liquor. When this odour hung in the air, I was always tempted to step back. But I never did, because these were friends who needed a hug or a quick conversation and would sometimes ask for prayers.

I recently reread the parable of the prodigal son, and it became personal to me. When I read of the father's passionate embrace of his son, I imagined that the odours of living with the pigs still clung to the son. But this didn't concern his father; he didn't step back but ran to embrace his son. He even called for the best robe to cover his son. His best covered his son's worst. This is what Christ does for each of us.

Prayer: *Merciful Saviour, thank you for the forgiving grace you constantly bestow on us. Amen*

Thought for the day: I can share Christ's love by embracing a friend.

Valerie L. Runyan (New Mexico, US)

PRAYER FOCUS: SOMEONE WHO NEEDS A FRIEND

SATURDAY 22 APRIL

Great Expectations

Read Psalm 103:1–12

Why do you look for the living among the dead? He is not here; he has risen!
Luke 24:5–6 (NIV)

When we read about the first Easter, we see that everyone except Jesus had expectations that were not fulfilled. Peter expected to remain loyal to Jesus. King Herod expected Jesus to perform a miracle. Pilate expected the mob to free Jesus rather than Barabbas (see Luke 22—23). The Jewish leaders who orchestrated the crucifixion of Jesus expected that the disciples would try to steal his body (see Matthew 27). The women who came to the tomb expected to anoint a dead body with aromatic spices (see Luke 24).

God exceeded all expectations at Easter. Jesus, through death and resurrection, created a bridge between humanity and God so that we may join God in joyful fellowship. We cannot reach God through our own efforts—by being good enough or earning our way. But God created a wholly unexpected way of salvation. We can come freely into God's presence because of what Jesus has done.

Prayer: *Dear Lord, we can never fully understand your ways, but we know you love us more than we can comprehend. Help us respond to your love and trust you in all circumstances. Amen*

Thought for the day: I live by faith, not by sight (see 2 Corinthians 5:7).

Jo Len Everhart (Idaho, US)

PRAYER FOCUS: SOMEONE LEARNING TO TRUST GOD

SUNDAY 23 APRIL

No Situation Is Permanent

Read Matthew 28:1–10

The angel said to the women, 'Do not be afraid, for I know that you are looking for Jesus, who was crucified. He is not here; he has risen.'
Matthew 28:5–6 (NIV)

In 2006, a man I worked with tried to have me killed for refusing to be his follower. He sent four young people to murder me at my home. All four were arrested before doing me any harm. I fled to Uganda, far from my family and friends.

Life in exile was hard. I spent nights without food, thinking about my family, who had no income for living or school expenses. During hopeless moments, I thought that God was no longer concerned with my prayers. Then I read Psalm 125:1–2: 'Those who trust in the Lord are like Mount Zion, which cannot be shaken but endures for ever. As the mountains surround Jerusalem, so the Lord surrounds his people both now and for evermore.'

The next day, a man from Colorado who was visiting Uganda asked to stay with me for a few days. After recognising the challenges I faced, he prayed with me and told me, 'In three days God can change everything.' This reminder of Jesus' miraculous resurrection comforted me. A few months later, my situation changed when I was admitted to Uganda Christian University to study theology. Today I am a pastor and a district leader in my denomination. God has the power to help us overcome challenging situations.

Prayer: *Loving Father, your power is beyond ours. Help us to trust your promises and look to you for help. In Jesus' name. Amen*

Thought for the day: When I trust in the Lord, I cannot be shaken.

Nzabonimpa Alexis (Kigali, Rwanda)

PRAYER FOCUS: THOSE WHO ARE PERSECUTED FOR THEIR FAITH

MONDAY 24 APRIL

All Equal

Read James 2:1–13

If you show partiality, you commit sin and are convicted by the law as transgressors.
James 2:9 (NRSV)

One of my earliest memories is of going to a restaurant for lunch with my parents. We sat at a table and the waitress handed us menus. However, to my surprise, a moment later we got up and walked out. I asked my mother why we were leaving since we hadn't eaten, and she pointed to a sign. I had not learned to read, but when we got outside, she explained that the sign said 'No Negroes Served Here'. 'That's not right,' my father said. He told me that we would not eat at a restaurant that would not serve everyone.

Segregation due to race is illegal now in my country. However, that doesn't mean racism is dead, and neither are other forms of discrimination. Whenever we show partiality to one person over another—whether due to manner of dress, level of income, nationality, race or any other factor—we discriminate. According to the verse quoted above, that's a sin.

As Christians, we live under the command to love our neighbours. Unfortunately, sometimes we consider our neighbours to be only those who are just like us. 'That's not right,' as my father said. Paul reminded the Galatians, 'There is neither Jew nor Greek… slave nor free; nor is there male and female, for you are all one in Christ Jesus' (Galatians 3:28, CEB). We are all equal in the eyes of God.

Prayer: *Dear God of the whole world, help us to see people through your eyes and to treat them in the same way that Jesus would. Amen*

Thought for the day: Those who are different from me are also God's children.

Tracy Crump (Mississippi, US)

PRAYER FOCUS: THOSE WHO EXPERIENCE DISCRIMINATION

TUESDAY 25 APRIL

Learning to Trust

Read Proverbs 3:1–6
The God of all grace, who called you to his eternal glory in Christ, after you have suffered a little while, will himself restore you and make you strong, firm and steadfast.
1 Peter 5:10 (NIV)

Ten years ago I came home from work one evening to find my home empty of all my possessions. My wife had left me, and I felt distraught. I began to question all my relationships, even my relationship with God.

When my divorce was finalised, I moved to the opposite side of the country. Once there, I never lived in one place for long and never kept a job for more than a year. I closed myself off from friends, family and from God. But no matter where I went or how much I avoided contact with people, my grandmother made sure I continued to receive copies of *The Upper Room*. And though I wasn't sure why, I continued to read the meditations, Bible passages and prayers. Maybe a small part of me still wanted to believe that while people may be deceitful, God's love indeed is honest.

Today, I have not completely moved on from my suspicions of relationships with other people, and I have not found all the answers to my questions about love and loss. But I have learned that while time might not heal all wounds, God does. I have learned to find joy in prayer. I'm beginning to think that continued faith in God's love is the answer.

Prayer: *Dear Healer of all wounds, help us to understand that while trusting in your love might not always be easy, your grace is real and active in our lives through any trial of faith. Amen*

Thought for the day: I can always believe in God's love.

Jason Dean Scott (New York, US)

WEDNESDAY 26 APRIL

The Gift of Serving

Read Numbers 8:14–22

The Lord said, 'I have given the Levites as gifts to Aaron and his sons to do the work at the tent of meeting.'
Numbers 8:19 (NIV)

For a couple of years, I helped in a crèche while parents were attending a church service. Each week, a dozen or more three-year-olds gathered in our room for songs, games and Bible lessons. I went home each week ready for a nap! I also went home filled with immense joy, knowing that I had helped to give parents a break and had taught energetic children about God.

All who do God's work need help. After the tabernacle's construction, God set apart the Levites to assist Aaron, the high priest. In the verse quoted above, God described these men as 'gifts to Aaron and his sons'. What an enormous help these men were to Aaron and the Israelites! They served in the daily duties of the tabernacle—sharing the burden of disassembling the tabernacle, carrying all its pieces when they moved camp and reassembling everything upon arrival at a new place. We can offer our local churches and Christian ministries the gift of service. Whether we teach, clean, greet people, set up a room or regularly pray for a ministry, God can use our work to help further the kingdom and to encourage our leaders. None of our gifts is too small.

Prayer: *Dear Lord, we offer our time as a gift to you today. Show us where we can further your work and serve you. Amen*

Thought for the day: What work has God called me to do?

Amelia Rhodes (Michigan, US)

PRAYER FOCUS: LEADERS OF CHILDREN'S MINISTRIES

THURSDAY 27 APRIL

Where Is My Focus?

Read Philippians 4:4–9

Whatever is true, whatever is noble, whatever is right, whatever is pure, whatever is lovely, whatever is admirable—if anything is excellent or praiseworthy—think about such things.
Philippians 4:8 (NIV)

During a period of time in my life I felt everything was going wrong. I became depressed and felt hopeless. God and his love for me seemed far away. I felt empty. When I shared my situation with my friends in faith, one friend gave me some advice. She challenged me to write down every one of God's blessings I experienced day after day—even the simplest ones. Every night I tried to think of three blessings God had given me that day. This discipline helped me tremendously. I found that God's blessings were gloriously abundant in my life. I had not recognised their presence because I was focusing only on my problems.

This experience of counting God's blessings has helped me to know that I can find joy even during difficult times. We can choose to focus on God and his blessings instead of only on our problems.

Prayer: *Loving God, in the midst of our struggles, help us to keep our focus on you and your eternal love for us. As Jesus taught us, we pray, 'Father, hallowed be your name, your kingdom come. Give us each day our daily bread. Forgive us our sins, for we also forgive everyone who sins against us. And lead us not into temptation.'* Amen*

Thought for the day: Instead of my problems, I will focus on God today.

Linawati Santoso (East Java, Indonesia)

PRAYER FOCUS: SOMEONE FEELING HOPELESS
* Luke 11:2–4, NIV

FRIDAY 28 APRIL

Flaws and All

Read Psalm 139:1–18

I praise you because I am fearfully and wonderfully made; your works are wonderful, I know that full well.
Psalm 139:14 (NIV)

When I was at high school, I was diagnosed with an eating disorder. For over two years, I despised my body. In this state it was impossible for me to believe that I had been created in God's image or that he loved me the way I was.

When I finally began my journey to recovery, I slowly began to understand that everyone has been created in God's perfect image. Through the years, I have learned that every single thing that God created is beautiful and wonderful, including each of us. We all have flaws and insecurities, but God doesn't make mistakes. The way we are is the way God intended us to be. So as we go through life, we try to remember that God loves us exactly as we are. His works are wonderful, and he loves and accepts us, flaws and all. With God's help, we can love ourselves and others as he loves us.

Prayer: *Gracious God, thank you for loving us and accepting us no matter what. Help us to remember that we have been created in your image and that your love for us is eternal. Amen*

Thought for the day: God loves me no matter what.

Ashley Oliver (Virginia, US)

PRAYER FOCUS: THOSE STRUGGLING WITH EATING DISORDERS

SATURDAY 29 APRIL

Prayer: A Gift of Love

Read James 5:13–16

Jesus said, 'Where two or three gather in my name, there am I with them.'
Matthew 18:20 (NIV)

During our weekly Bible study at church, one of the members asked if anyone would be interested in coming to the prayer group next week. I never gave much thought to joining the group because I don't consider myself a 'prayer warrior'. As I began to think about prayer, I wondered if I could be sincere in praying for others, especially people I don't know. However, I do know that when I need God's help in my life, I stop and pray, knowing that he will guide me through any situation. If I pray for God's blessings on my life, why not pray for others too?

As I asked God for guidance about joining the prayer group, a passage of scripture came to mind: 'Love your neighbour as yourself' (Matthew 22:39). I realised that prayer fits with this commandment: I can show love for others through praying for them. As I continued to recall scripture verses, I remembered that James 5:16 tells us to pray for each other, and Matthew 18:20 tells us that when we gather together in Jesus' name, he will be there with us. Through scripture, God gave me the encouragement I sought to attend our church's prayer group.

By praying for others, either alone or with a group, we show them love. Prayer is indeed a way to 'love your neighbour as yourself'.

Prayer: *Loving God, as we pray for others, may they know your powerful, loving presence in their lives this day and always. In Jesus' name. Amen*

Thought for the day: Today I will demonstrate love through prayer.

Jim McCullough (Ohio, US)

SUNDAY 30 APRIL

Diamonds in the Rough

Read Ephesians 3:14–19

Jesus said to Paul, 'My grace is sufficient for you, for my power is made perfect in weakness.'
2 Corinthians 12:9 (NIV)

One misty, grey morning I went walking with my children just as the rain stopped. We passed a drab, bare field of roughly mown stubble. Returning some time later, however, we were witnesses to an amazing transformation. The clouds had cleared and the sun was shining. Over the entire field of stubble were thousands of cobwebs covered with droplets of water. They sparkled in the light like diamonds. It appeared as if the entire field were covered in diamond lace. It was beautiful.

My parents recently celebrated their diamond wedding anniversary (60 years). Those closest to them know that, throughout their marriage, life has not always been easy, much less perfect. But we also recognise and celebrate that their faithfulness and devotion to God has brought a transformative and wonderful covering of grace to their lives.

Jesus promises that his grace is sufficient for us and is, in fact, made perfect in our weakness. When at times we feel like our lives are like dry stubble, we can take heart in knowing that his love, mercy and grace cover us and that we too are made whole, precious and beautiful in his sight.

Prayer: *Dear Lord, you make all things beautiful in your time. Give us eyes to see what you see. Amen*

Thought for the day: What dry area of my life needs Christ's covering grace?

Marion Palmer (South Australia, Australia)

PRAYER FOCUS: TO BECOME CLOSER TO JESUS

Small Group Questions

Wednesday 4 January

1. How often do you share your faith with another person? What is the experience of sharing your faith like for you?

2. Would you describe yourself as a patient person? In what parts of your life could you become more patient?

3. The writer says, 'Opportunities to share our faith present themselves in daily life, often unexpectedly.' Can you think of a time when this was true for you? How did you react to the situation?

4. Why do you think 'fishing' is a good illustration for sharing our faith with others? Are there other images that come to mind?

5. With whom in your daily life could you share your faith today?

Wednesday 11 January

1. Have you ever been asked by a person you do not know well to pray for him or her? How did you pray for this person?

2. What do you do when you try to pray but cannot find the right words?

3. How frequent are your prayers throughout the day? Are there certain times of day you like to pray? In particular locations?

4. Some people may not be comfortable offering a prayer aloud and in public. Can you think of a time when you were asked to pray aloud in the company of others and were not comfortable doing so? How did you respond?

5. What does scripture teach us about prayer? What does it say about how we are to pray and how often?

Wednesday 18 January

1. When have you started something that you had to stop and then start over? Can you see any parallels between this experience and your life of faith?

2. What types of small-group gatherings does your community of faith offer? Do you participate in any of these gatherings?

3. What challenges do you face today? What stories from scripture encourage you when you are facing challenges?

4. Do you think the challenges that confronted the early Christians in the New Testament were greater than those we are confronted with today? Why or why not?

5. What new opportunities to serve God can you take advantage of today?

Wednesday 25 January

1. Recall a time when you endured a sorrow or a loss. What sustained you during this experience?

2. What questions have you asked God during difficult times? Did God answer your questions? If so, how did you feel about God's answer?

3. Name some characters in the Bible who experienced great grief and loss. How did they approach their circumstances? What can we learn from them?

4. The writer says, 'Only prayer and scripture brought answers to my soul: deep, unspoken answers that gave me joy in the midst of sorrow.' What do you think she means by 'unspoken answers'?

5. How does your faith community support people who are grieving? What does your community do particularly well? What could your community do better?

Wednesday 1 February

1. What does the Bible say about trust? How do those verses or stories influence your trust of other people? How do they help you trust God?

2. Have you ever had a difficult time trusting someone at first but over time learned to trust them? Describe the situation and what it was that eventually helped you trust them.

3. Who do you identify with more in this meditation, Shorty or Shorty's family? Explain your answer.

4. Is there ever a time when a person is beyond redemption? Yes or no? Why?

5. Who are the physically, mentally, emotionally and spiritually broken in your community today? What specific actions can you take to make them feel safer and more loved?

Wednesday 8 February

1. Can you think of someone in your own life who, like Bill, is always willing to help others? Why are people like Bill so important in our lives of faith?

2. Have you ever done a good deed for another person for which you received no credit or return? How did this make you feel?

3. Why does God give each of us different talents? What talent would you like to have that you do not? What talent do you have that you are grateful for?

4. Name some people in your community who offer their gifts and talents freely to others. Who are they, and what gifts and talents do they offer?

5. What gifts do you offer your community of faith? What other gifts could you offer? What gifts do others in your community contribute that you especially appreciate?

Wednesday 15 February

1. Why might it be easier for us to put our trust in money or power instead of God?

2. Can you think of an instance in which you placed your trust in something other than God? What was the outcome of the situation? What did you learn from it?

3. The writer says only God can 'guide us to true freedom'. What do you think 'true freedom' in God means? What would 'true freedom' in your life look like today?

4. What characters in scripture experienced 'true freedom'? What parts of their story can you apply to your life?

5. Sometimes family demands, work and other responsibilities can distract us from God. What practices help you to keep God the focus of your life?

Wednesday 22 February

1. Do you think God is more likely to grant our prayer requests when many people are praying? Why or why not?

2. What are your expectations about the way God should respond to your prayers? How do you respond when God doesn't answer your prayers the way you would hope or expect?

3. What threatens your prayer life? What sustains and strengthens it?

4. Does God value some prayers more than others? Explain your answer.

5. Where did you learn to pray? Who taught you how to pray? What memories do you have of your early prayer life?

Wednesday 1 March

1. Who through their perseverance, courage, and dedication has inspired you along your faith journey? In what ways have they inspired you?

2. Do you observe Lent by taking on a new discipline or by giving up something? What do you get out of the experience?

3. Name something that you could give up this Lent in order to grow in Jesus' likeness. Name something that you could take on. Which of these do you think will best help you grow closer to God?

4. How can you relate to Matt's statement, 'It is easy to be a fan but hard to be an athlete'? Can you think of an instance in your life during which you found it easy to be a fan but hard to be an athlete? Describe the experience.

5. What disciplines or habits do you practise in your life of faith that help you grow closer to Christ?

Wednesday 8 March

1. Think of a story from scripture where God has given someone new life. In what ways do you relate to the story? How does it encourage you?

2. How does Lent help us prepare the soil of our lives for the new things that God is doing within each of us? Why is 'preparing the soil' important?

3. Do you sense any new and exciting challenges on the horizon for your growth as a Christian? If so, what are they? How are you preparing for these challenges?

4. What spiritual disciplines—prayer, scripture reading, meditation—do you practise that help cultivate the soil of your life? How do these disciplines make you more aware of and ready to receive the new life God offers?

5. Where have you seen signs of new life around you in the past week? What were they? In what places and in what ways will you look for signs of new life in the days and weeks to come?

Wednesday 15 March

1. What 'strangers' can you think of from scripture? How do their stories help us better to understand our relationship to God and to one another?

2. Has there ever been a time when you were in a strange place or situation and others welcomed you into the group or community? What was this experience like for you? What did it teach you about yourself and about others?

3. How easy or difficult is it for you to talk to someone different from yourself? Why is it easy or difficult?

4. Name some of the barriers—social, political, ethnic, economic, religious—that exist between people. What do you believe God thinks of these barriers? As Christians, how should we respond to the things that separate people?

5. Who are the strangers in need of welcome in your community? What can you do to make them feel welcome?

Wednesday 22 March

1. What is the most difficult situation you have faced in your life? Describe the situation. What got you through it? What did you learn from it?

2. Have you ever felt invisible while enduring a hardship? How did this experience change the way you look at others in similar circumstances?

3. Name some characters in the Bible who faced seemingly insurmountable obstacles. Describe their situations. How did they overcome their obstacles? What can we learn from them?

4. How did you respond to the last homeless person you encountered? After reading today's meditation, will you respond differently to the next homeless person you meet? Why or why not?

5. For what challenges and difficulties do you need Christ's strength today? What scripture passages do you rely on for inspiration and encouragement?

Wednesday 29 March

1. When have you given to someone expecting nothing in return? What was this like for you?

2. Jesus says, 'For the measure you give will be the measure you get back.' What did Jesus mean by this statement? Can you think of a specific situation from your own experience that illustrates what Jesus was talking about?

3. Why is it important for us to give to others out of our abundance? Is giving to others easy or difficult for you? Why?

4. Recall a gift that was given to you for which you were unable to repay the giver. How did this make you feel? Did it change the way you give to others? If so, how?

5. Name one gift you can give in the coming week. What is the gift? Who will you give it to?

Wednesday 5 April

1. What spiritual leftovers do you serve to God? Why do you think he wants us to give our fresh spiritual selves each day?

2. What is the first thing you do in the morning after getting out of bed? How might it change your day to do something entirely focused on God—praying, studying scripture, reading a meditation—upon first waking?

3. Think of a time when you have not given God your best. What was the outcome? What would you have done differently?

4. What activities keep you from spending time with God? What things in your life can you let go that would allow you to focus more closely on him? What would letting go of these things cost you? How would it benefit you?

5. Name some of the blessings God has given you today. How do you show him gratitude for these blessings? In what new ways can you show God gratitude?

Wednesday 12 April

1. When was the last time you showed mercy to another person similar to the way in which the Samaritan showed mercy to the man? Describe the situation. What did this teach you?

2. When was the last time you were in a time of crisis and someone was a Good Samaritan to you? Who was your Good Samaritan? What did this person do to help you?

3. What in the story of the Good Samaritan challenges you or makes you uncomfortable? Why?

4. Have you encountered someone in need of help, but instead of helping the person you passed them by? Reflecting on this experience, how do you feel about your actions now? What could you have done differently?

5. What does it mean to you to be a neighbour to others? Who needs your help? What can you sacrifice to help this person?

Wednesday 19 April

1. Have you prayed for someone but the outcome of their situation was different from what you were praying for? What does this say about prayer?

2. Do our prayers make a difference in the lives of those for whom we are praying? What difference would it make in your life if you knew someone was praying for you?

3. It has been said that 'Prayer doesn't change God, it changes us.' What do you make of this statement? Do you think it's true? Can you think of a time when you have been changed by prayer?

4. Try to recall instances in scripture when Jesus prayed for others. What can Jesus' prayers for us teach us about our own intercessory prayers?

5. Who in your faith community needs your prayers today? What in your own life do you need others to pray for?

Wednesday 26 April

1. When have you felt that your gifts were too small to make a significant contribution to the work of your church?

2. Have you ever tried to do something alone but discovered you could do it only with the help of another person? What were you trying to do? Who helped you accomplish your task?

3. Who in your church contributes their gifts to improve the well-being of the congregation? In what ways can you show gratitude to these people for their service?

4. Why is the gift of service important? Why do you think God wants us to use our gifts to serve others?

5. Name some of the opportunities to serve in your faith community. To which of these opportunities could you offer your gifts and talents?

Share it with a friend!

We conducted a survey to see what our readers think of *The Upper Room* and why they read it. It was encouraging to hear of the positive impact *The Upper Room* is having on your lives. Often it started because someone recommended, shared or gave a gift of *The Upper Room* to you.

Would you considering sharing a copy with a friend or family member?

Here are some ways you could share your experience of BRF's Bible reading notes:

- **Recommend:** We'd like to encourage you to talk about *The Upper Room* and the readings that have particularly spoken to you. Maybe someone will consider picking up a copy, so that it can have a positive effect on their life too.

- **Give it:** It's really easy to set up a gift subscription for any of BRF's Bible reading notes. To find out more, just go to our web page (**www.biblereadingnotes.org.uk/subscriptions**) or speak to our Customer Services team on +44 (0)1865 319700.

- **Start a group:** If you order five or more copies of our Bible reading notes, you can set up a group subscription and save money, as you pay no postage and packaging charges.

- **Donate a copy:** When you've finished with your copy, give it to your local church or to someone who can make use of it.

Journal page

Journal page

Journal page

Journal page

Journal page

Journal page

Journal page

Journal page

Explore the freeing, life-changing nature of forgiveness. As we move from Ash Wednesday to Easter Day, daily reflections and prayers help us to experience the living power of the cross of Christ through biblical and modern-day stories of wrongdoing and forgiveness.

The Living Cross
Exploring God's gift of forgiveness and new life
Amy Boucher Pye
978 0 85746 512 2   £8.99
brfonline.org.uk

Stepping into Grace finds powerful connections between the call and mission of Jonah and the mission context of our own time. Using the narrative thread of the biblical story to explore themes of ambition, vocation, spirituality, mission, leadership and personal growth, it argues for a ministry rooted in grace, where who we are becoming in Christ provides a foundation for our participation in the mission of God.

Stepping into Grace
Moving beyond ambition to contemplative mission
Paul Bradbury
978 0 85746 523 8 £7.99
brfonline.org.uk

The life stories of the Celtic saints are inspirational. They demonstrate great and unassuming faith, often in the face of insurmountable difficulties. In *40 Days with the Celtic Saints* David Cole draws us to relate our own life journey and developing relationship with God into the life story of the Celtic saint of the day. A corresponding biblical text and blessing encourages and motivates us to transform our lives for today's world in the light of such historic faith.

40 Days with the Celtic Saints
Devotional readings for a time of preparation
David Cole
978 0 85746 548 1 £7.99
brfonline.org.uk

God's Belongers should transform our thinking about what it means to belong to church. David Walker replaces the old and worn division between 'members' and 'non-members' with a fourfold model of belonging: through relationship, through place, through events, and through activities. From his extensive practical research, the author shows how 'belonging' can encompass a far wider group of people than those who attend weekly services. This opens up creative opportunities for mission in today's world.

God's Belongers
How people engage with God today and how the church can help
David Walker
978 0 85746 467 5 £8.99
brfonline.org.uk

How to encourage Bible reading in your church

BRF has been helping individuals connect with the Bible for over 90 years. We want to support churches as they seek to encourage church members into regular Bible reading.

Order a Bible reading resources pack
This pack is designed to give your church the tools to publicise our Bible reading notes. It includes:

- Sample Bible reading notes for your congregation to try.
- Publicity resources, including a poster.
- A church magazine feature about Bible reading notes.

The pack is free, but we welcome a £5 donation to cover the cost of postage. If you require a pack to be sent outside the UK or require a specific number of sample Bible reading notes, please contact us for postage costs. More information about what the current pack contains is available on our website.

How to order and find out more
- Visit **biblereadingnotes.org.uk/for-churches**.
- Telephone BRF on +44 (0)1865 319700 Mon–Fri 9.15–17.30.
- Write to us at BRF, 15 The Chambers, Vineyard, Abingdon OX14 3FE.

Keep informed about our latest initiatives
We are continuing to develop resources to help churches encourage people into regular Bible reading, wherever they are on their journey. Join our email list at **biblereadingnotes.org.uk/helpingchurches** to stay informed about the latest initiatives that your church could benefit from.

Introduce a friend to our notes
We can send information about our notes and current prices for you to pass on. Please contact us.

Subscriptions

The Upper Room is published in January, May and September.

Individual subscriptions
The subscription rate for orders for 4 or fewer copies includes postage and packing:
The Upper Room annual individual subscription   £16.50

Group subscriptions
Orders for 5 copies or more, sent to ONE address, are post free:
The Upper Room annual group subscription   £13.20

Please do not send payment with order for a group subscription. We will send an invoice with your first order.

Please note that the annual billing period for group subscriptions runs from 1 May to 30 April.

Copies of the notes may also be obtained from Christian bookshops.

Single copies of *The Upper Room* cost £4.40.

Prices valid until 30 April 2018.

Giant print version
The Upper Room is available in giant print for the visually impaired, from:

Torch Trust for the Blind
Torch House
Torch Way
Northampton Road
Market Harborough   Tel: +44 (0)1858 438260
LE16 9HL   **torchtrust.org**

THE UPPER ROOM: INDIVIDUAL/GIFT SUBSCRIPTION FORM

All our Bible reading notes can be ordered online by visiting biblereadingnotes.org.uk/subscriptions

☐ I would like to take out a subscription myself (complete your name and address details once)
☐ I would like to give a gift subscription (please provide both names and addresses)

Title .... First name/initials .... Surname ....

Address ....

.... Postcode ....

Telephone .... Email ....

Gift subscription name ....

Gift subscription address ....

.... Postcode ....

Gift message (20 words max. or include your own gift card):

....

....

Please send **The Upper Room** beginning with the May 2017 / September 2017 / January 2018 issue (delete as appropriate):

Annual individual subscription ☐ £16.50   Total enclosed £ ....

Please keep me informed about BRF's books and resources ☐ by email ☐ by post
Please keep me informed about the wider work of BRF ☐ by email ☐ by post

Method of payment

☐ Cheque (made payable to BRF)   ☐ MasterCard / Visa

Card no. ☐☐☐☐ ☐☐☐☐ ☐☐☐☐ ☐☐☐☐

Valid from M M Y Y   Expires M M Y Y

Security code* ☐☐☐   *Last 3 digits on the reverse of the card
ESSENTIAL IN ORDER TO PROCESS THE PAYMENT

Please return this form with the appropriate payment to:
BRF, 15 The Chambers, Vineyard, Abingdon OX14 3FE

To read our terms and find out about cancelling your order, please visit brfonline.org.uk/terms.

The Bible Reading Fellowship is a Registered Charity (233280)

UR0117

THE UPPER ROOM GROUP SUBSCRIPTION FORM

All our Bible reading notes can be ordered online by visiting biblereadingnotes.org.uk/subscriptions

☐ Please send me .... copies of ***The Upper Room*** May 2017 / September 2017 / January 2018 issue (*delete as appropriate*)

Title .... First name/initials .... Surname ....

Address ....

.... Postcode ....

Telephone .... Email ....

Please do not send payment with this order. We will send an invoice with your first order.

Christian bookshops: All good Christian bookshops stock BRF publications. For your nearest stockist, please contact BRF.

Telephone: The BRF office is open Mon–Fri 9.15–17.30. To place your order, telephone +44 (0)1865 319700.

Online: brf.org.uk

☐ Please send me a Bible reading resources pack to encourage Bible reading in my church

Please return this form with the appropriate payment to:
BRF, 15 The Chambers, Vineyard, Abingdon OX14 3FE
To read our terms and find out about cancelling your order, please visit **brfonline.org.uk/terms**.

The Bible Reading Fellowship is a Registered Charity (233280)

UR0117

To order

Online: **brfonline.org.uk**
Telephone: +44 (0)1865 319700
Mon–Fri 9.15–17.30

Delivery times within the UK are normally 15 working days. Prices are correct at the time of going to press but may change without prior notice.

BRF

Title	Price	Qty	Total
The Living Cross	8.99		
Stepping into Grace	7.99		
40 Days with the Celtic Saints	7.99		
God's Belongers	8.99		

Please complete in BLOCK CAPITALS

POSTAGE AND PACKING CHARGES			
Order value	UK	Europe	Rest of world
Under £7.00	£1.25	£3.00	£5.50
£7.00–£29.99	£2.25	£5.50	£10.00
£30.00 and over	FREE	Prices on request	

Total value of books	
Postage and packing	
Donation	
Total for this order	

Title .... First name/initials .... Surname..

Address..

.... Postcode ....

Acc. No. .... Telephone ....

Email...

Please keep me informed about BRF's books and resources ❏ by email ❏ by post
Please keep me informed about the wider work of BRF ❏ by email ❏ by post

Method of payment

❏ Cheque (made payable to BRF) ❏ MasterCard / Visa

Card no. ☐☐☐☐ ☐☐☐☐ ☐☐☐☐ ☐☐☐☐

Valid from [M M] [Y Y] Expires [M M] [Y Y] Security code* ☐☐☐
Last 3 digits on the reverse of the card

Signature* .... Date ..../............/............

*ESSENTIAL IN ORDER TO PROCESS YOUR ORDER

The Bible Reading Fellowship Gift Aid Declaration

giftaid it

Please treat as Gift Aid donations all qualifying gifts of money made
❏ today, ❏ in the past four years, ❏ and in the future **or** ❏ My donation does not qualify for Gift Aid.

I am a UK taxpayer and understand that if I pay less Income Tax and/or Capital Gains Tax in the current tax year than the amount of Gift Aid claimed on all my donations, it is my responsibility to pay any difference.

Please notify BRF if you want to cancel this declaration, change your name or home address, or no longer pay sufficient tax on your income and/or capital gains.

Please return this form to: BRF, 15 The Chambers, Vineyard, Abingdon OX14 3FE | enquiries@brf.org.uk
To read our terms and find out about cancelling your order, please visit **brfonline.org.uk/terms**. UR0117
The Bible Reading Fellowship (BRF) is a Registered Charity (233280)

This page is left blank for your notes.